Cutting Edge Connections in Today's Classroom

Teaching Above and Beyond Tradition

Rosemary Dolinsky

Cutting Edge Institute LLC,
Publishers
888-718-3170

publishwithcuttingedge.com

This book is dedicated to:

Vincent

Acknowledgments

Special thanks to:

My husband, Billy, for his support, endless guidance and help steering me into my right direction.

My twin daughters, Kristen and Jill, whose belief in me helped me to believe in myself.

Joe Renne, Elena Healey, Roselyn and Bob Colletti, St. Isabel Farza, FMA, who gave me the courage to venture into the consulting world.

Meira-Leah Scott, my editor, for her patience, diligence, competence, and sense of humor in the face of pressured deadlines.

Finally, to Vincenzo and Maria Yuppa who instilled in me the importance of education, pride, determination, and taught me to "always reach for the impossible."

Foreword

It is a thrill for me to introduce you to my friend, Rosemary Dolinsky. I have known Rosemary for many years and have watched her grow and evolve as an educator, national facilitator, educational consultant and author. I think that the most important thing we can learn from her is TO BE A NO LIMIT TEACHER.

She is constantly researching the most recent, cutting edge methods to inspire educators to be the best they can begin their schools and/or classrooms. Rosemary believes when educators are true to their profession, they are happier and more productive. Thus, they are more open to give their students the compassion, understanding, and the love which they deserve.

She stresses the key to being successful teachers is knowing that what we are doing for our students has no limits; that we, as educators, must continue to stretch and grow. It is then and only then our students will also stretch and grow.

I know you have chosen the perfect guide in Rosemary to show you how to accomplish this!

Elena Healey

BA, MA, M.Ed

Table of Contents

~1~

Introduction

What if you no longer had to imagine the perfect classroom, that is, one in which every child was working to his or her potential and discipline problems were non-existent? What if I also told you that you could be on the brink of creating an almost perfect educational atmosphere by using simple cutting edge strategies in your classroom based on research in the areas of neurology, psychology, music and, believe it or not, the marketing industry?

Sounds too good to be true, right?

As an educational consultant, national workshop facilitator and graduate instructor, my many years of research allow me to introduce theories prevalent in one discipline to another field to create new possibilities that enhance the educational experience of practitioners and students alike. For instance, as I was discussing the physiological impact smells and color have on the brain to my Brain Compatible Strategies in the Classroom graduate class, a student piped up, *"Your information sounds so convincing, however, no one ever mentioned this to me in any of my other classes. I'm curious. How did you come up with that?"*

Good question, but not surprisingly, the answer involved another question I had often asked myself as an educator: *"How do we reach every child's brain in a classroom full of children knowing that every child is different?"*

Fortunately, my role as an educational research consultant allowed me to stumble on research that I realized had tremendous implications for the teaching field. Current studies in physiology demonstrate that the brain reacts to colors, scents, sounds, visuals, timing, and emotions.

Think about this: Artists choose certain colors to create desired moods; designers influence the environment to calm or stimulate us; and, marketing companies spend millions of dollars researching color for packaging.

In fact, these companies even understand the marketing impact of using the "right" scents in products. They also know the "magic" number needed to etch a product in the consumers mind. Simply put, they are masters at creating an ad campaign to appeal to all individuals. By asking clients to bake cookies, brew coffee, or have a fire burning when potential buyers visit, even real estate agents understand the importance of creating an emotional "tag" of comfort when selling a home.

Now, if artists, designers, marketing agencies, and even real estate agents can manipulate "the brain" through the environment, it dawned on me that educators, who are responsible for molding of our world through our children, could also understand these "manipulations."

Hence, my proposition that the "imagined" world of the perfect classroom is a closer reality than many of us ever thought.

(A) **Ask yourself:**

1 • Do I know which students in my class are auditory, kinesthetic or visual learners?

2 • Do I post upcoming events within peripheral vision range to activate subconscious curiosity?

3 • Do I know the personality styles of each of my students?

4 • Do I know each student's hemispheric preference?

5 • Do I use music during the day to stimulate or calm my students?

6. • Do I make use of particular smells in my classroom to stimulate particular moods?

7. • Do I make an effort to use particular colors on my bulletin boards to stimulate particular physiological reactions?

8. • Do all my students have water to sip on throughout the day?

"Fix the Tires"

If you answered "no" to any of the above questions, then it is time to "think outside the box" and realize that teaching is not just about covering the core curriculum. If we view teaching as a vocation and the means by which we can enhance the skills of others so that they maximize their potential in the world, then teaching must extend beyond the textbook.

To accomplish this goal, teaching must, therefore, combine focused lesson planning with the application of physiological research. This research performed outside of the educational world understands the workings of a child's brain and the means through which we can access the process by which each child integrates knowledge.

To continue using the conventional approach to teaching with this kind of research at hand, is not unlike rolling on your rims in an accident instead of simply fixing the flat.

Let me explain.

Picture yourself in a car with four flat tires. You have two choices. The first is to continue along the road with those four flat tires and arrive at your destination hours or days later than you intended, assuming the rims don't give way and prevent you from arriving at all. The second is to get out of the car, fix the tires and live with the certainty that you will arrive at your destination as planned because you addressed your problem "head on."

It was this simple message that convinced my graduate students, and it is the one that I present to you in this book: "Get out of the car and fix the tires" in your classroom by using the cutting edge strategies I share with you in this book to reach the true goals of the teaching profession.

You may find this time consuming, but I promise you that your initial effort will payoff in the long run by helping your students arrive at their destination which will in turn help you accomplish your objective as a teacher. And, as an added bonus, you will prepare your students to continue learning well beyond your classroom.

They will learn how to become life-long learners!

~2~

The Presentation

I am an educator who seeks to make available to other educators the latest and most cutting edge strategies I can find that fulfill the real potential of the teaching profession and are practical and easy to implement in the classroom. These strategies are based on the well documented scientific and teacher action research I have been fortunate to explore as an educational research consultant. My goal is for educators to create successful learning environments for the student of the 21st century.

My mission puts me in front of teachers, principals, and superintendents. I shuttle from coast to coast presenting my workshops or stay close to home when I am teaching a graduate course. My audience varies in size from the few to the thousand plus range. Writing this book is my way of putting down on paper the material I have been presenting to the wonderful educators I have had the privilege to meet, many of whom have become personal friends.

Sometimes, when I notice a young teacher in my audience, I have a flashback to the beginning of my career in education. Admittedly, back then, even I would never in my wildest dreams have thought I would be doing what I am doing today. I began teaching in 1972 and I loved it! What a rush I felt when my students "got it." However, as time went by, the strategies I had once used with success were no longer as effective as they had been. I knew I needed to "tweak" my style. So, I began to focus on learning styles, brain research, personalities, and multiple intelligences, learning centers, creativity and differentiated instruction.

These new and "cutting edge" theories gave me the motivation plus the permission to experiment in my classroom.

And...the passion returned!

After receiving my Masters of Education degree, I stayed in the classroom and began teaching graduate school as an adjunct instructor on a part-time basis. One day, I was asked to present what I knew about brain research to a group of local teachers. Soon, I was instructing local educators on the implications of brain research for teaching professionals. I continued teaching middle school, graduate school and presenting workshops on my days off from the classroom.

The feedback from my graduate students and workshop participants regarding these studies was amazing. Teachers were using the strategies and techniques I presented with wonderful success. In fact, many teachers told me they were able to improve communication with a difficult student just by being open to and trying new ideas that were based on what they had learned from my presentations. And, isn't making a connection with a child who had seemed "unobtainable" what teaching is all about?

The defining moment of my life's direction occurred approximately five years ago after I taught my first graduate class and presented my first workshop. My administrator handed me my evaluation. Her words defined my destiny. She wrote, "*I am concerned about your trying to accommodate each student's individual learning style in your teaching. I want you to keep in mind that there is a core curriculum to cover when you conduct your lessons.*"

Then and there, I knew it was time to move on. It was time to convince others on a deeper level that the only way we can accomplish amazing results in our classrooms is to use the documented physiological studies and techniques that had been used with success in marketing and other fields. It was time to persuade educators to incorporate these techniques into the teaching profession. Also, it was time to encourage educators to accommodate the unique learning style and personality of every student in the classroom in a manner that accomplished the level of results seen daily in other fields.

My story met the receptive ears of two administrators, Ms. Walsh and Mr. Caputo, from Pennsylvania. Indeed, Ms. Walsh appeared visibly upset and commented that a chill went up and down her spine when she learned that there were still administrators whose approach to teaching was as rigid as that of my former administrator.

Mr. Caputo went as far as to declare that addressing different learning styles is a major component of effective teaching in the classroom. Both principals were emphatic that every avenue to enhance the learning experience of students will remain open to the students under their watch. Parents whose children attend their schools can be rest assured that Ms. Walsh and Mr. Caputo are willing to incorporate new teaching strategies based on physio-logical research on a constant basis to their faculty. Their response assured me that there was a supportive audience for what I had to say and that I should waste no time relaying my message as an educational consultant.

The Cutting Edge Workshop
Pre-Presentation

My life as an educational consultant often takes me on the road. There, I not only teach the cutting edge principles for revolutionizing traditional education to educators nationwide, but I also incorporate them into the actual presentation. I always arrive at the workshop site early. Despite the number of presentations I have performed, I still get a thrill looking over an empty room knowing that, shortly, it will be filled with the sounds of curious educators who have come to hear me speak. The customary goal of many workshop participants is to take at least one practical strategy back to the classroom. Nevertheless, I always hope my participants will be sufficiently inspired to retain many of the strategies I present for their classroom use.

I try to greet my participants as they enter the meeting room and talk to as many people as I can before the presentation commences. I listen closely to what they say. Are they using action, visual, or hearing words? This is important because listening carefully to an individual's choice of words, gives me a strong indication of his or her preferred learning style. I always scope the room to identify the unique learning styles of workshop attendees.

I note the people who have their legal pads at hand and are ready to record important information. These people are what I call Periods or Question Marks: the Sequential Learners. I observe the participants who strike up conversations or walk around the room. These are the Interpersonals and Kinesthetics. I mentally note where these people choose to sit.

Just as I teach the importance of recognizing students' styles, I also must recognize the individual styles of my students—the participants. I must know right from the start that the lady wearing the blue sweater needs me to make eye contact with her when I speak and that the gentleman in the beige shirt wants me to present an overview of the workshop. My audience is no different from your students. They represent a mixture of learning styles and personalities. My job in a presentation and your job in the classroom is the same.

And, this is the message that I present to you today: Learn the strategies that I teach you here, and you can adapt them to any learning environment and experience the ultimate connection between student and teacher. I incorporate these strategies myself at every workshop event no matter how basic they might be. For instance, I remind myself that in order for cognition to occur, I must meet the primary need of every human being - survival.

I, therefore, conduct a series of seemingly administrative tasks that in actuality have strategic physiological and educational objectives. I check the temperature of the room. The room can't be too hot or too cold. I glance towards the food table to check the availability of coffee, snacks and water.

Something as simple as a full urn of water plays an important role in the work I plan to do. My goal is to enhance cognition, and water keeps the brain hydrated and its electrical impulses connecting smoothly and efficiently.

Once I am satisfied the survival needs of my participants will be met, I focus on meeting my audience's emotional needs. I commence by contemplating the strategies I will use to bond with my participants and make them feel safe. It is mandatory that I establish their trust and make them laugh to release their endorphins. Endorphins are naturally occurring chemicals in our brain that promote happiness. By tapping into this substance, I can create a natural bonding mechanism among a large group of people.

Breathing deeply for a moment or two, I embark on another technique to use the physiological strategies I have learned to enhance my own cognitive abilities and workshop success: I relax close my eyes, and create a visualization: *In my mind's eye, I see myself presenting my workshop and anticipating any questions I may be asked. I practice the answers I will give. I envision the conclusion of the workshop. It was wonderful. The participants had a great time and I inspire them so much they want more!*

Creating this visualization is a powerful strategy. I do so by:

- Practicing my presentation

- Rehearsing my response to questions

- Having set my goal for success

After creating the visualization, I have no doubt that the day will unfold any way other than how I saw it in my mind. As you attempt the same in your classroom, remember this: Your brain has difficulty knowing the difference between mind visualization and reality. It believes what you are telling it to be true!

By keeping this in mind, if a child approaches you and says, "I can't do this." Your response as one who has mastered this process should be along the lines of, *"Honey, your brain believes what you tell it is true. It is your best friend. If you tell it you can't, then you won't. In fact, as Henry Ford once said, 'If you think you can or think you can't, you're right.' Tell yourself that you can, and I promise you, YOU WILL SUCCEED!"* This visualization process may be a difficult concept to grasp initially, but I have tested it over the years and know that it's tried and true.

Now…with my visualization complete, there is usually just enough time before the workshop begins for one quick glance at my outfit. My appearance is as essential as the look of my presentation materials. Indeed, the attention I give to my clothes is no less intense than the thought process that goes into my choice of wrapping for my workshop handouts. My clothes are how I package myself and, like all packaging, it has a physiological impact. A red scarf draped over a black suit conveys a message that is distinct from a pair of denim overalls. Red, for instance, conveys a message of high energy and stimulates interest and excitement.

Since the emotions evoked are intuitive, it hardly matters that my audience is unaware of this fact. The suit as a choice of clothing conveys yet another message. My decisions regarding colors and scents may be determined days or weeks before a workshop to accomplish a calculated physiological and psychological effect on my audience.

A whiff of vanilla scented perfume will have a predetermined effect on my audience by activating certain neural activity in the front area of a participant's brain. My audience, of course, is unaware of my subtle manipulations. However, they will learn all about these manipulations by the end of the workshop, as you, too, will learn about them by the time you have finished this book!

Before I begin to speak, I am usually struck by how perfectly still my audience is sitting and how intently they are focusing on me as I approach my "stage position." I can read the anticipation in some faces, and I sense the "prove it to me" attitude in others. I clear my throat and…

THE PRESENTATION BEGINS!

~3~

The "Learning Styles" Connection

Recently, I presented a workshop in the Midwestern section of the United States. My participants had just completed a visual (i.e. mind map) and a brief introduction about their lives. One particular individual showed the group her picture and began her story by telling us about her hectic lifestyle. She explained, *"After teaching each day, I help my husband on our hog farm."*

Now, I was born and raised in the New York metropolitan area. I don't know any one who owns a hog farm, and I have never been to a hog farm. At first blush, I could only think of pig waste and the stench that had to linger under one's nose hours after working with farm animals. It wasn't my idea of a restful evening. In reality, my idea of a certain lifestyle doesn't make hers wrong. It just makes hers different. My participant's experience would have me recuperating in a hospital ward for weeks.

This story had a major impact on me. Even those steeped in educational theories need to recognize their ongoing application.

This experience compelled me to relate it to the continuing need for teachers to be understanding, accepting, and patient with respect to the different ways in which people learn.

Why is this so important? Because teachers tend to teach in their comfort zone! If a teacher is a visual learner, he or she will use more pictures or charts with emphasis on color in presentations.

If a teacher is an auditory learner, he or she will tend to lecture or focus on classroom "conversations." If a teacher is a kinesthetic learner, his or her lessons will be more "hands on."

Unfortunately, when teachers use techniques strongly based on their learning preference, some students in the classroom won't connect to the subject matter the teacher is presenting. What is more disturbing is that such students are often unfairly labeled as being unintelligent.

In reality, there is a strong possibility that such students simply do not have the tools to study and learn in ways that are conducive to maximizing the potential that lies within their individuality. Or, maybe the teacher is merely using strategies not geared to the preferred learning styles of these students when presenting a lesson in the classroom.

As a workshop presenter, it is important for me to remind teachers there is no right or wrong style of learning. There are just different styles. I emphasis this point with what has become my "signature" statement of my message:

It is not right or wrong, it just is.

What Are Learning Styles?

Everyone learns in different ways. Just as we like different types of music, have different friends or wear different clothing, we also prefer learning in different ways. As an educator, it is essential for you to address learning styles with your students and teach them strategies that are available for each style. This can empower students and assist them in taking responsibility for their own learning. Your students will then work "smarter not harder."

A personal learning style is nothing short of a sensory preference. Students develop a preference over time for one sense over another to gather and process information from their environment. In other words, they lean on one particular sense to represent most, but not all of their sensory experience.

Once you arm yourself with strategies designed specifically for each sense preference, such as using auditory skills instead of visual skills, learning in your classroom will become a **faster and easier** process for each student.

To understand how each of your students prefers to learn, it is **NOT** necessary for you to give them the formal written assessment that I have included in this section.

All you need to do is **LISTEN** to your students when they speak and **OBSERVE** their behaviors.

Listen to Your Students' Vocabulary

Each style has its own distinct vocabulary. Since we tend to use language that connects with our style, vocabulary gives you a real starting point for determining whether your student is (1) an auditory learner who learns best by listening, reading aloud, and talking; or (2) a visual learner who learns best by watching, visualizing or drawing, or (3) a kinesthetic learner who learns best by doing and moving. You can ascertain the differences by listening to the vocabulary that your student uses.

Students who rely on listening, the **Visuals**, use "picture" words such as:

- I can **VISUALIZE** it.

- I can **PICTURE** it.

- I can **SEE** that.

- Let's **FOCUS** now.

Students who rely on their auditory senses to learn, the **Auditories**, rely on "sound" vocabulary:

- **TELL** me.

- That's **CLEAR as a BELL**.

- Can you **HEAR** what I mean?

- Can we **TALK**?

- That **SOUNDS** right.

Students who use movement as a means of learning, the **Kinesthetics,** may be heard using "moving" phrases:

- I'd like to **GET** a better idea of this information.

- I have a **GUT** feeling about this.

- Let's **TOUCH BASE** later.

Recognizing a visual, auditory, or kinesthetic learner by observing your students is also another way to analyzing without testing. My audience is always amazed at my ability to identify learning styles without a formal test. But, I explain I use no tricks. There are just certain traits you should take note of which will quickly and easily tip you off to individual styles.

Observing and Working with the AUDITORY Learner

The auditory learner may raise his or her hand or approach you to repeat information you have just told the class or the directions you have just given. Without knowing this is a basic auditory learning strategy, it is possible for a teacher to believe that this child is not paying attention or is confused. In reality, this student may be an auditory learner and is merely putting information into what is known as "Elaborate Rehearsal." Elaborate Rehearsal is a paraphrasing technique to help the brain make a connection to an outside stimulus.

I recall a workshop presentation I made some years ago. After I explained the paraphrasing learning technique to the audience, a middle school teacher, Mary Beth Resin, raised her hand to tell us how her graduate instructor had become annoyed with her because she would frequently stop the lecture just to repeat what was being said in class. Mary Beth rarely asked a question. She just needed to paraphrase what she had just heard. She explained: *"I realized many years ago this was a strategy I must use when I processed a new piece of information. My dominant learning style is auditory and, finally, my technique has been validated in this workshop. I won't feel intimated next time I stop another lecture."*

Ironically, the graduate class Mary Beth was talking about was a class on learning styles! Auditory learners often have difficulty with written directions. So, it stands to reason a class that is dedicated to accommodating the learning style of the Auditories will require reading the directions to a test or assignment aloud before letting the class work independently.

By doing this, you can be almost 100% positive that the auditory learner has as much chance of comprehending the directions as the visual learner has from reading them.

The following technique is one of my personal favorites to reach the auditory learner. After presenting information for a few minutes, stop. *Tell your students to turn to each other and repeat what they just heard you say or what they just learned in the last few moments.*

To make this "stop, turn and talk" strategy more effective, ask them to stand and discuss the information with their classmates in their immediate area. By this method, you have not only reached the Auditories, but you have the students moving which will keep them alert and focused which helps the cognitive process.

The auditory learner may move his or her lips while trying to remember information or during silent reading. Don't be put off by such behavior. Remember, this is a learning strategy. Auditories need to hear the information in order to remember it, and the lip moving is a form of "hearing."

The information will then have a better chance to be stored into the student's memory. Auditory learners enjoy listening, talking, and have outgoing personalities. They love to tell stories and their stories are very descriptive. These learners usually solve problems talking about them. In fact, out of all the learning styles, auditory learners are the most talkative.

REMEMBER...AUDITORY LEARNERS LEARN BEST BY:

• Listening.

• Reading Out Loud.

• Talking.

Teach the auditory learner in your classroom to:

1. Make tapes of classroom notes and listen to them when studying.

2. Read notes, directions, or other information out loud.

3. Work with a friend so he or she can talk and listen to the course material.

4. Create jingles to help remember.

5. Ask questions in order to hear more information.

6. Create flashcards for studying and read them aloud.

Observing and Working with the KINESTHETIC Learner

Locating the kinesthetic learner is easy. This student is quite the opposite from the auditory learner. The Kinesthetic is a poor listener. It is difficult for the kinesthetic learner to be placed in a lecture type setting or even engage in a conversation to remember information. Because their listening skills are not strong these students need to be taught how to take excellent notes since they will be relying heavily on them during study sessions.

The student who prefers the kinesthetic learning style needs to "move" or "do" while learning. This is the student who is swinging the leg, tapping the pencil or drumming fingers on the desk. Also, this is the student who is bobbing the head or swaying the body while studying silently. I know that pencil tapping, finger tapping, and excessive body movement can be very annoying to the teacher. However, rather than being annoyed, think about these body movements as a signal from which you can learn. Through body language, this student may be saying to you: ***I'm ready to learn!***

Instead of asking the student to stop what he or she is doing, consider making the entire class stand up and ask them to take a stroll around the classroom while discussing the course material with each other.

Kinesthetics do not have internal pictures of organization. In fact, Kinesthetics tend to be very unorganized. These are the children who need strategies to remember books, homework and class schedules. These students, in particular, need to be taught how to take excellent notes since they will be relying heavily on them during study sessions. Besides taking notes on class information, Kinesthetics would benefit from your asking them to summarize daily activities in their notebooks as a study aid.

Creating a "movement/show me" activity to remember vocabulary, information, or directions is an excellent strategy for the teacher to relay to kinesthetic learner.

Let me give you a few examples, and then you can adapt them to your situation.

I Move Learning Activity

I handed an assignment to my Styles of Personality graduate class. As part of the assignment, I asked them to read a section silently, discuss specific questions with the cooperative group, and create a mind map of the information. I then directed them to create an activity for each part. The specific directions were as follows:

Direction One: **Read**

This required students to open their books and pretend to read.

Direction Two: **Discuss**

Students were instructed to open and close one of their hands to make a "talking" Signal.

(3) Direction Three: **Create a mind map**

This step required each student to use one of their fingers to draw an imaginary picture in the air.

Once the students had followed these directions and created the signals, I asked them to **TELL** me and **SHOW** me the assignment   simultaneously. The students followed this instruction as directed. Interestingly, they were not only able to do this, but *NO ONE QUESTIONED THE ASSIGNMENT!*

Let's take this type of activity into a lesson you may teach.

Give the students a list of vocabulary words. It could consist something related to science, social studies, literature, or, indeed, any subject. Then, divide the class into groups and have each group create a group signal representing each word on the list. Next, ask each team to define an item on their list without using words. In other words, group members cannot talk. They can only SHOW what the word means. If you like, you may ask another team to determine a word from another team's signal.

Elizabeth Gallardo, a teacher at John Paul II School in Clifton, NJ, tried and loved teaching vocabulary using this method. In fact, she relayed excitedly,

"In the past I have found I it difficult to teach vocabulary to a second grader. However, this year, I related the word to a movement of the body. It was a problem solver. My students did wonderfully on their vocabulary test. With this strategy, 95% of the class passed all given vocabulary tests."

A Pennsylvania high school teacher named Bonnie Miller used this same activity to teach a sequence of web designing in her computer classes. All she did was have the students create motions that corresponded to the design steps they had to remember. Bonnie told me that the success rate her students had in terms of remembering the information jumped "through the roof."

Try using this extremely powerful strategy by asking your students to create motions to represent settings in literature, history, steps to follow doing science experiments, or math concepts.

I remember teaching place value to my students. We created a conga line and sang, "One, two, three, comma" as we danced around the room.

Tell your students to show you an acute, obtuse, or right angle by drawing in the air. Better still, have the students actually create the angles with their bodies. There is no end to what your students can "show you."

REMEMBER… KINESTHETIC LEARNERS LEARN BEST BY:

- Moving

- Doing

Teach the kinesthetic learner in your classroom to:

1. Walk or stand when studying.

2. Act out information.

3. Chew gum while studying.

4. Design learning games.

5. Underline important information in a textbook or in their notebooks.

6. Build a project to explain an idea.

When you incorporate strategies to meet the needs of the *"I need to move"* students, you are really doing a tremendous service to every student in your classroom regardless of preferred learning style.

According to Linda Hemmat, who is an A.F.A.A. National Certified Trainer, movement is the key to delivering oxygen to the brain which is the food our brain needs to carry out our tasks. She encourages bursts of exercise which she calls "dynamic movement" of any duration or degree of intensity for children to keep their supply of oxygen flowing.

In fact, Linda cautions teachers to watch for signs of yawning which is an indicator of decreased "oxygen uptake." This decrease in oxygen uptake can lead to lethargic behavior.

Ms. Hemmat's advice has been confirmed in a recent study stating oxygen administration to the brain results in improved cognitive performance, including, memory formation and, specifically, word recall and reaction time.

Observing and Working with the VISUAL Learner

There really isn't any concrete explanation as to why the visual learning style is the most dominant style. Over 60% of our population leans towards being visual learners. Maybe it's because today's society depends heavily on visual clues: video games, computers, TV, movies and books.

Whatever the reason, it is extremely important to develop strategies to accommodate visual learners in the classroom. I am a strong visual learner. My research on physiological studies and the strategies I have developed were based on these studies, have helped me understand why I did not do as well on exams when the classroom was in a large lecture hall. Classes held in this type of environment cater to the auditory learner!

Visual learners are easy to spot. They sometimes have their eyes closed or seem to be staring "up" into space. No, they are not sleeping or daydreaming! They are probably creating a picture in their mind that is connecting to what you are saying.

You can use student "mind pictures" to your advantage. As you are teaching, pause. Ask your students to close their eyes and picture themselves standing in front of an imaginary chalkboard.

Then, ask them to create a doodle on their imaginary chalkboard which shows a picture of the information you have just presented. *(To add a kinesthetic strategy, tell them to also draw their "mind picture" in the air with their finger as they are "seeing" it on their imaginary chalkboard.)*

Visual students have vivid imaginations and learn very well when they create mind maps or doodle their mind's pictures on paper as others are talking. Visuals actually think as if there were a video or digital camera in their mind.

I once asked my class to create directions from the classroom to the principal's office. I told them to write the directions on paper in any style they found comfortable. I provided this assignment as a simple strategy to help me identify my visual learners. These students would probably be the ones who handed the directions to me in picture form. *Which is, by the way, exactly how I write directions?*

Using video equipment is important to visual learners. If you can create Power Point or Publisher presentations for your lessons, you will be using a powerful technique to reach to visual learners. Using color in your presentations is a necessity when working with Visuals. What are some other techniques you can use? You could ask your students to create a pictorial booklet of events in history, science objectives, or story plots from literature. Have the students draw the pictures or cut pictures from magazines for the booklets.

Let me ask you a question. Have you ever removed information from the classroom wall or bulletin board for an examination? Did you ever notice that during the examination some students stared at the section of the wall or bulletin board where the information used to hang?

As I present my workshops, I always move to another area of the room when I begin a new topic. Throughout the day, I deliberately move back to that section of the room where I had previously presented information. Then, I ask the group to recall whatever I was talking about when I stood there. There are ALWAYS people who know exactly what I had said while standing on that spot. Trust me. It happens every time. This is a wonderful technique to use in your classroom.

I have a particular concern regarding the visual student who needs locational clues where the information has been taught to stimulate recall when taking tests. This is a learning technique for some students that has been extensively overlooked! If this is a significant learning aid for over 60% of our population who represent visual learners, doesn't it make sense to test such students in the same classroom in which the initial learning occurred?

Aren't we putting the visual students at a serious disadvantage when they are tested in a different room? To do so, is to take away the visual triggers these students need to access the information they have learned.

REMEMBER... VISUAL LEARNERS LEARN BEST BY:

- Seeing.

- Mind Picture.

- Drawing or Creating a Picture.

Teach the visual learner in your classroom to:

1. Change the color of ink in pens.

2. Look at all the pictures and charts in a chapter before reading.

3. Draw pictures of what they see in their minds while reading.

4. Use highlighters when reading or taking notes.

5. Close their eyes to visualize what is being discussed.

6. Visualize facts or word spellings while trying to memorize.

The following is a simple test for you to determine the learning styles of individual students. Why not give the test to your class? This will also help each student to better understand his or her learning preference and create personal techniques to make learning faster and easier.

What Kind of Learner Are You?

Directions: Circle the items that describe you best. Try to focus on your answers to the questions and ignore the letter designation until the end of the exercise.

1. If I am learning how to do something new, I would rather:

    (V) Talk about it.

    (A) Read about it.

    (K) Create something with my hands related to the topic.

2. While reading, I often:

    (V) See pictures in my mind of what I am reading.

    (A) Read out loud to understand the information.

    (K) Fidget while I am reading.

3. When I tell someone how to do something, I:

    (V) Like using pictures to explain the information.

    (A) Have no trouble explaining the directions orally.

    (K) Gesture with my hands as I am talking

4. When I am unsure of a spelling word, I:

   (V) Write the word on paper to see if it looks right.

   (A) Spell it out loud to hear if it sounds right.

   (K) Write the word in the air before I write it on paper.

5. While doing a report, I:

   (V) Pay attention to how well spaced my letters and words look.

   (A) Say what I want to write out loud.

   (K) Push hard on my pen as I am writing.

6. When my teacher is presenting a lesson, I like her to:

   (V) Use the board, overhead projector, or show pictures during a lesson.

   (A) Talk using lots of expression in her voice.

   (K) Use hands-on activities.

7. I have trouble remembering when:

   (V) The room is messy, or there are people moving around.

   (A) The room I am in is very noisy.

(K) I have to sit at my desk for any length of time.

8. When I solve math problems: I:

(V) Use drawings to see the problem.

(A) Talk myself through the steps.

(K) Move objects or use my body to help me think.

9. When I am given instructions on how to put something together, I:

(V) Look at the pictures and try to see where the parts fit.

(A) Read the directions out loud, and talk to myself as I put the parts together.

(K) Put the parts together without reading the directions and then read later.

10. When I have nothing to do, I:

(V) Look around, stare, or read.

(A) Like to listen to other people's conversations.

(K) Walk around and touch things with my hands.

11. When I am giving an oral report, I:

    (V) Usually am quick because I don't like talking.

    (A) Go into detail because I like to talk.

    (K) Use gestures and like to move around/shift my body while I am talking.

12. When someone is talking to me, I:

    (V) Try to see what she is saying in my mind.

    (A) Enjoy listening, but want to interrupt and talk myself.

    (K) Become bored if the report gets too long and detailed.

13. When trying to remember a person's name, I remember:

    (V) The face but not the name.

    (A) The name but not the face.

    (K) Where or when I met or learned about the person but not the name or face.

14. When I take a test, I:

    (V) Can see my notes or information in my head.

(A) Can hear the teacher's lesson in my mind.

(K) Can remember hands on assignment to recall the information.

Now total the number of letters corresponding to each answer.

V_____ A_____

K_____

The abbreviated letters designate different learning styles:

The letter "V" refers to the visual learning style; the letter "A" to the auditory learning style; and the letter "K" to the kinesthetic learning style.

The letter that corresponds to your highest number will indicate your learning style preference.

~4~

The "Scent" Connection

Ever opened the door of a new car?   Oh, that smell!

Don't you love it? When the smell wears off, there's no need to pine for your loss. There are actually sprays available to replicate this "new car" smell. This keeps the love going between you and your car!

Do you recall the experience of walking into a bakery? The aroma hits you as soon as you enter. Your eyes wander to all the goodies and you probably linger longer than you usually would have on a shopping errand. Maybe the smell even makes you buy more than you should.

How does this happen? It's probably because you associate the smell of the cookies, cakes and pies to good times in your life. You might be reliving the experience of baking cookies with your mom or grandmother. Or, perhaps, the aroma reminds you of happy birthdays? Maybe you picture yourself eating and drinking cookies and milk just before bed, a time when you felt safe and content?

Personally, I just need to catch a whiff of tomato sauce simmering on a stove and I return to the Sunday afternoons where for so many years I shared dinner with all my aunts, uncles and cousins at my Grandparents' home. What good times that smell brings back to me!

There is a well-established physiological reason why smell evokes an emotional memory. However, before I get ahead of myself and talk about the brain, olfactory, emotional connection, and memory, I would like to share with you why I find this area of study particularly exciting. Did you know that the information scientists have revealed regarding the impact of smell on memory has currently been used just about everywhere BUT education?

It is for this reason I am absolutely excited at the possibilities this information can bring to education, and the contribution this book can make in introducing its underlying concepts to other educators. Hopefully, after reading this chapter, this information will also excite you!

The research and techniques that I disclose to you will allow you to experiment with what is today known as **_Environmental Fragrancing_**. A concept that has gained popularity for its effect in many other disciplines.

The growing knowledge of smell and its influence on brain activity has propelled my initial curiosity into something tantamount to a full-blown obsession! I am constantly searching for new research connecting smell to learning and trying to discover which companies use smell in the workplace, or why perfume makers have chosen a particular scent to market.

Knowing what I know now, I believe it is important for those in decision-making roles for educators to understand the powerful connector smell can be to memory. I hope there will be an understanding how technological advances using smell can relate and promote success in the classroom. It is then, and only then, we will more likely see some serious "cutting edge" use of smells in our schools.

Indeed, I can recall teaching a workshop in Massachusetts, where I met James C, special education instructor. James was a marketing agent prior to becoming a teacher. At the workshop, James told me:

> *"In one of my college marketing courses, the class read and discussed how different retail businesses put millions of dollars each year into discovering how scent affects people. This included department stores looking for scents to put in the air circulation systems to stimulate parts of the brain that would make a customer more likely to purchase products. It also included the practice of movie theaters circulating the air toward the front door so that the consumer's first smell would be that of popcorn."*

Given my fascination with this area of physiological study, imagine the thrill I experienced meeting this participant.

What a perfect research contact!

Scent in the Corporate World

The Japanese have been actively researching Environmental Fragrancing since the 1970's. Shimizu Corporation, one of the largest construction companies in the world, has worked in conjunction with Takasago, Japan's largest fragrance company, to create and patent a system that disperses a pre-set scent plan into the workplace. The density of the scents fluctuates as an attention grabber. Shimizu disperses peppermint into its offices and conference rooms. This aroma was chosen because peppermint is supposed to increase work efficiency, lessen mental fatigue, and eliminate drowsiness. (More about this later!)

The new headquarters of Kajima, another construction company in Tokyo, has a beautiful atrium with a brook, fountain, and 25 different species of trees. Every ten minutes, their environmental fragrance system emits aromas. The scent and density of these smells varies depending on the time of day, temperature, humidity, and seasons of the year.

It is important to point out that these scents are released on a level that is so subtle and difficult to detect that they virtually operate subliminally. Since smell is associative, not everyone is going to like each scent. Therefore, to obtain the maximum effect, employees of these companies were asked to complete surveys asking for their reactions to particular aromas. The surveys continued over the course of one year.

At Kajima, a typical day would begin with the morning wake up call of a refreshing citrus scent. At midday, the system changed to a floral scent to enhance concentration and inspire work. After lunch, the cycle repeated itself starting with citrus scents followed by that of florals. At the end of the workday, wood scents, which promote relaxation, were circulated into the air so that the employees left the workplace in a calm state.

By the way, the Tokyo Stock Exchange is fragranced every afternoon with peppermint to make the brokers feel invigorated and refreshed. Don't forget, this is a place where fast thinking pays off!

One of the companies that markets scent dispensers is a London based company. This company claims that potential buyers should purchase the dispenser to:

- Enhance product ranges by introducing their specific aromas.

- Improve the overall atmosphere and browsing time and store loyalty

- Affect shopping behavior.

- Support and enhance specific promotions.

- Create an ambiance in public areas, such as hotels, clubs, pubs, etc.

• Neutralize and eradicate unwanted odors.

The company even creates a company logo or corporate identity with a signature fragrance!

The Environmental Fragrance system has found strong support in Professor Shizuo Torii from the Toho University School of Medicine in Japan, and his research on the reaction of brain waves to scents. However, the fascination with scents and their impact on brain functions started way before the 1970's when Dr. Torii recorded his findings.

Let's take a look at some of the historical beginnings of the research associated with scent and the brain, starting with action research.

The Beginnings of Scent Research

In the 1920s, two Italian physicians, Renato Cayola and Giovanni Gatti, published "The Action of Essences on the Nervous System." The doctors' goal was to discover if there was any effect of smell on the opposing states of depression and anxiety. To determine the answer to this question, they either sprayed aromas into the air or applied aromas to a cotton wool pad or applied the pad directly to the face using a mask. The doctors measured the changes in blood pressure and depth of breathing in the candidates under study.

The results were intriguing! They concluded that the sense of smell has, by reflex action, an enormous influence on the function of the nervous system. The odors they identified to stimulate, and, thereafter, use for depressive states, included: angelica, cardamom, lemon and fennel. The odors they identified as relaxers, which were subsequently used for anxiety states, included: chamomile, melissa, neroli, petitgrain, opoponax and valerian.

Many years later in 1980, Dr. Jean Valnet published "The Practice of Aromatherapy" which explained his successful application of aromatics in the treatment of psychiatric patients between the 1950's and the 1970's. In his work, he used pine, basil, and sage as stimulates and lavender, lemongrass and marjoram as anti-spasmodics.

Professor Paolo Rovesti of Milan University took up research in this area in the 1970's. He measured the restorative effect of aromas on a patient suffering from anxiety or depression. He found lemon, orange, verbena, jasmine and sandalwood to be most effective with depression. To relieve anxiety, he used lime, lavender, neroli, petitgrain and bergamot. According to Rovesti, it is also important for the smell to be pleasing since the brain tends to reject unpleasant odors.

In 1962, Dr. R. W. Moncrieff carried out the first systematic study using an EEG monitor to measure brain wave activity and the effect of fragrance on the brain. He found that odors could change EEG levels. Thus, Dr. Moncrieff paved the way for later developments in this area such as those by John Steele.

In 1979, Steele began some experiments using a portable multi-channel EEG, called a mind mirror, to evaluate the effects of various smells on the brain's rhythm patterns. As exactly predicted, Steele found that the cephalic oils (which stimulate mental clarity and memory) such as basil, rosemary, black pepper and cardamom, induced beta predominant patterns. Beta brain rhythms are correlated with aroused attention and alertness. At the other end of the spectrum, the floral antidepressant euphorics such as neroli, jasmine and rose induced an unusual amount of delta rhythms with some alpha and theta present.

Professor Torii, whom I mentioned before, initiated a research program to study the reaction of brain waves to scent, and it was then that interest in environmental fragrances truly began! During each of Professor Torii's experiments, his subject had electrodes attached to his scalp which showed the "normal" EEG trace. The measuring device was an electrical brainwave pattern created by anticipation. This measuring device is called CNV curve. The tests results were true to what the Professor has expected! The EEG was suppressed by lavender and increased with jasmine. Lavender calmed and jasmine stimulated. And, from here on, the brain's reaction to smell became a real challenge in the scientific community!

Having explored this research, I posed this question to myself:

If the time has come to apply human alertness technologies to the workplace, why not schools?

I believe that you, too, are now thinking about smell and the impact of Environmental Fragrancing in our schools.

However, I don't believe I have yet "fixed the tires" and fully educated you as to the significance of smell, the brain, and its influence on learning.

To this end, it is time I turn to the experts for additional assistance.

Dr. Alan Hirsch, a neurologist and psychiatrist, is also the founder and Neurological Director of Chicago's Smell & Taste Treatment and Research Foundation. In addition to the evaluation, diagnosis, and treatment of disorders related to smell and taste, the Foundation's research extends to the effects of odors and flavors on emotion, mood, behavior, and disease states. Additionally, Dr. Hirsch is the author of more than 100 articles on the psychological power of scent and four best selling books on scent research.

In his book, "Life's a Smelling Success: Using Scent to Empower Your Memory and Learning," Dr. Hirsch states that: "There is a strong overlap between the anatomic and neurochemical structures for olfaction and for memory." He continues to explain how this works: "Once they are up the nose, the odor molecules reach the olfactory epithelia, the smell center located just behind the bride of the nose. The epithelia are mucous coded membranes about the size of a dime. As the odor molecules move through the thin membrane, they reach a pin-sized area where millions of receptor sites are located. These receptor sites allow us to distinguish between odors and identify them.

The body's electrical system is involved because neurons fire off an indication that a particular odorant is present. The odors signal travels through the cribriform plate, a paper-thin part of the skull through which olfactory nerves are projected from tiny hole. When the odor molecule reaches the olfactory bulb, which is in the brain itself, it is intensified by a factor of about 1,000. In other words, the brain intensifies and transforms the molecule a thousand times in order to respond to the odor. Obviously, this process happens so rapidly that we do not experience it step by step, nor are we conscious of it. The mechanism by which an odor is intensified is what allows us to detect about 10,000 different odors.

What is more fascinating is the fact that the sense of smell works opposite from all the other senses. The brain recognizes all the other stimuli before we decide if we like it or not. In the case of smell, the brain decides whether it likes it or not before it recognizes it."

This explanation is one of the reasons that I was so excited about the sense of smell and its implications for teaching. Unlike the other senses that may be more intuitively understood to have an impact on learning, our sense of smell is distinct from the way in which our other senses operate.

Dr. Hirsh elaborates on the speed with which we react to odors:

"When you detect an odor in the air that affects you emotionally, it may take few seconds to understand why you are sad or happy or perhaps distressed or disturbed in some way."

The Link between Memory and Smell

Now that we have learned how smell interacts with our brain, for the purpose of this book, I would like to expand this concept to discuss the link between memory and smell. This relationship may stem from how our brains evolved. Early sea animals could detect chemicals in the water because they had sensors on their outer bodies. These sensors may have evolved into senses of taste and smell. Connected to the sensors was a small lump of nerve tissue cells that may have helped the sea animals decide which path to take or which path to avoid.

Many scientists believe that the modern animal brain developed, in part, from these bundles of nerve tissue cells. Today, this part of the brain, known as the limbic system, remains pretty much the same as it was in the time of the sea animals. This section of the brain is called the "old brain" for these obvious reasons. The "old brain" contains our emotional and pleasure centers. Unlike sight, hearing and touch, smell travels directly to the limbic section of the brain.

Now, here lies the connection between memory and smell:

The hippocampus, where short term memory connects with long term storage, shares the same nerve pathways that are shared by the sense of smell! This is why a strong memory stored in the hippocampus can be triggered by a smell recognized in the emotional area of our brain. And, more importantly, we are now seeing that using the sense of smell can help to store the learning episode into the part of our brain that governs long-term memory.

By the way, I am sure the word aromatherapy popped into your mind as you were reading. There is yet another word that is used for an established area of scientific study that explores the relationship between psychology and scent. New York's Fragrance Institute coined this word. The word is **aromachrology.**

Let's take a look at some aromachrology that has been going on with scents.

• A Japanese research study measuring the impact of aromas on keyboard operators showed that they made 20% fewer errors in the presence of lavender, a stress reducer, 33% fewer errors with jasmine, a relaxer, and an AMAZING 54% fewer errors when lemon, a stimulating aroma, was circulated in the air.

• Remember the peppermint? In a study at Wheeling Jesuit University in West Virginia, athletes ran faster and did more pushups when exposed to the scent of peppermint than when exposed to other scents or no scents at all. So, dabbing some peppermint oil on your collar may boost your mood and help you perform better.

• A prominent cancer center diffused a vanilla like substance in one of its MRI tubes to reduce stress. The patients reported a lower anxiety rate. Unfortunately, the doctors who began this research left the center and the testing ended.

To add a slightly different perspective to the research I have presented, I found an extremely interesting bit of advice for men offered from a men's health website:

> *"The key to using cologne is this: Women have a stronger sense of smell than men. To smell just right, spray the fragrance into the air, then walk through the mist. On a first date, try cologne that's just hit the market. That way, you don't have to worry about reminding her of her ex-boyfriend."*

There's the emotional tag again!

I have saved a report on an incredible technological advancement for the end of this chapter. A California-based company has created a device that connects to your computer and prints out smells received online. Although the company admits that the smells are "not exact" copies of the real thing, it claims the product can create "thousands" of scents commonly found in cosmetics, foods and beverages.

Why would you want to have this gadget on your computer?

Possibly for scented email or sampling aromatherapy, groceries, cosmetics, and home care products before purchase. I can imagine that new car smell being sent over the computer lines while searching the internet for good prices and locations for your new car.

By this time, I am sure I have convinced many of you that scent has been overlooked as a necessary component for the educational environment. So let us take our research and apply it to the classroom. I must begin with a few warnings. If you use scent in the classroom, please remember:

- It is important to check medical records for students who may have any allergies towards scent.

- Candles should not be used.

- Use scents subtly. The scents should be learning enhancers not distracters.

- Never spray scents directly on the children. If possible, spray the air freshener into the air preferably about 15 minutes before the children enter the room.

- Otherwise, there are no limits to your using scents creatively in your classroom or school.

In your classroom...how about:

- Adding scent to finger paint, use scented markers or provide scented stickers as rewards.

- Since lemons promote alertness, why not have students write new letters and words using lemon juice or actually have the students write the words on real lemons! You could also instruct your students to write math facts with the lemon juice or directly on the lemons!

• Stringing citrus flavored cereal for counting or using the strings to create patterns?

• Citrus flavored cereals come in different colors. Why not use these different colors to practice sorting?

• Drinking lemonade is a fun way to begin "serious" work such as math or a test.

• Fill the air with the scent of cinnamon crackers or cinnamon air freshener. The students will know it is time for social studies! Do they smell basil or sage in the scent pot? It must be time for journal writing.

Following is a summary of different scents with their potential outcomes:

ALERTNESS

• Peppermint

• Lemon

• Eucalyptus

• Pine

• Basil

- Cintronella

- Grapefruit

REFLECTION/RELAXATION:

- Jasmine

- Lavender

- Tangerine

- Sandlewood

- Mint

- Majoram

- Chamomile

- Cedarwood

- Honeysuckle

CREATIVITY

- Rosemary

- Rose

• Cinnamon

• Sage

• Apple

• Ginger

On the next page is a chart to help you match scent and the classroom activity.

ACTIVITY	SCENT
Introducing new learning Reinforcing difficult concepts Keeping students' attention	Fruity smells or wood smells
Working on reflections Performing learning assessments Quiet activities	Florals or soft spices
Performing creative activities Connecting new learning to old learning	Strong spices, strong apple, or rose blends

I would like to share with you the activities one of my Brain Compatible Strategies in the Classroom graduate students created in her classroom to use the power of scent to produce an effect other than alertness, relaxation or creativity. She wanted the students learn the course material using their sense of smell to create the necessary association in the brain between information and memory. She did so by creating *"smell bags!"*

Kristina wanted to teach her class about products from different sections of the country, so she gave each student one of the brown paper bags and a specific section of the country as an assignment. She then instructed each student to draw a map of his or her assigned area and place a sample of a product produced in that area into the bag. For example, if a student had been assigned Idaho, he or she might place a potato into the bag. Next, she asked the students to seal the bag and poke holes in it so the scent of the product could escape.

One teacher's inspiration can be the source of inspiration for other educators teaching different subject areas. For example, another teacher loved Kristina's idea and thought this would be great to teach historical events. This teacher had the students create bags that represented what the Pilgrims might have smelled while crossing on the Mayflower! This idea is something that you can really run with!

My questions to you…have I convinced you of the importance of the smell connection? **I HOPE SO!**

~5~

The "Music" Connection

Music has been with each of us since conception. For nine months, we lived with the rhythmic beats of our mother's heart. After birth, we live with the rhythmic beats of our own heart and the tempo of our own body. Music is a universal language. With music, we don't need linguistic skills to communicate with those from another country! Music entertains, changes mood, creates friendships, communicates, entertains, energizes, and inspires creativity.

Throughout history, music has been an important reflection of a society's culture. To paraphrase Confucius: *"If you want to know how well a people are governed, if its laws be good or bad, examine the music it practices."*

In fact, during the Renaissance period, music ranked in equality with arithmetic, geometry, astronomy as one of the four areas of important learning. Aristotle himself was a firm believer in music education.

Music and Research

Unfortunately, with so many budget cuts in education today, music is usually one of the first programs administrators eliminate from school curriculums. Ironically, by cutting music from schools, we may be doing away with an essential gateway to improving the reading, math and science skills of our students.

Today, considerable research is being conducted to explore then very question of whether music is, in fact, a window into higher brain function. Preliminary findings appear to indicate that it is. From as far back February 19th, 1996, Newsweek Magazine wrote an article titled "Your Child's Brain" which stated: *"When children exercise cortical neurons by listening to classical music, they are also strengthening circuits used for mathematics. Music excites inherent brain patterns and enhances their use in complex reasoning tasks."*

According to Advanced Brain Technologies: *"The extraordinary universal principle of entrainment natural synchronization of heart rate, brain waves, and breath to external periodic rhythm is fully grounded in medicine, biology, and physics using EEG."*

Music is Brain Based Learning at its Best!

Music is a perfect fit with every learning style. It is for the Auditories (I hear) and the Kinesthetics (I move). With the addition of a songbook or lyric sheet, music is for the Visuals (I see) style. Music establishes "meaning and sense" and, thus, becomes an effective strategy for cumulative learning and recall.

Marketing agencies have recognized the power of songs and jingles for years. Most TV commercials are based around music. I am sure most of you can list the ingredients of a Big Mac, ("two all beef patties, lettuce, cheese, pickles, and onions on a sesame seed bun"), by singing the popular jingle associated with this food. Or, you can tell me the product that comes to mind when you hear: "Plop, plop, fizz, fizz…Oh, what a relief it is!" (Alka-Seltzer.)

Music involves emotional connections. It can lift a spirit on a rainy day and reduce the stress of academic pressures. Music is calming and is known to have a soothing effect on student behavior.

A Belleville, New Jersey teacher, Deborah Weyland, attended one of my Key Techniques to Strengthening Student Learning workshops, which describes experiences based on brain based learning. At that workshop, I spoke passionately about music.

Approximately three weeks after the workshop, Deborah emailed me. She wanted to tell me what had happened after she began playing music while her students entered the classroom. Deborah wrote: *"I thought I would give this technique a try and see what would happen."* She continued: *"I chose different types of 'quiet music.' Sometimes the songs were classical selections since I wanted to expose my students to this genre of music. Other times, I chose my favorite 'soft rock' music without any lyrics. After about one week of this daily 'entrance music,' I really noticed a difference in how my students entered the room. They were not as chatty or unfocused as they had been. In addition, I was spending less time having to refocus the group so they could start my lesson. What an amazing disciplinary strategy!"*

Ms Weyland created a positive atmosphere conducive to learning for her students. She also made her job much easier at the start of each class period!

Music and Brain Waves

Brain waves and breathing! These are words that we do not readily associate with music. Nor do we associate these words with classroom management or retention of learning objectives into long term memory. But understanding that there IS a link between brain waves, classroom management, breathing, and recall ability might encourage you to try your own action research with music in the classroom!

As your brain listens to music, electrical energy is released by the neurons and creates brain waves. These brain waves are either in Alpha, Beta, Theta, or Delta states. The brain state produced will determine what your body is best prepared to do at any particular moment. A state could speed up or slow down the electrical energy produced by the way in which it reacts to the tempo (beats per minute) of a song.

Before you play background music, you must therefore be aware of two things. First, it is important to know approximately how many beats per minute there are in a particular song. To determine the number of beats per minute, play your selection.

Once you feel comfortable that you have the beat, watch the clock and count until a minute has passed. This will give you a good estimate of the number of beats there are per minute. Secondly, when choosing songs to play before or during teaching periods, you must determine your goal for the lesson.

One the next page is a chart to help you differentiate between brain states and determine the beats per minute associated with each state and the type of activity it is most likely to elicit. After reviewing the chart, you may want to create your list of songs for class or school activities.

Do you want creativity (writing), higher level thinking skills, concentration or problem solving? Once you set your goal, you are ready to choose the appropriate musical selection.

Ideally, you should select music within the range of beats per minute that corresponds to the Alpha state. This is the brain state that works best to stimulate most educational experiences.

The music compositions of Bach, Handel, Vivaldi, Corelli, and Manteverdi fit in this category as does much Native American music, the Japanese bamboo flute or any music with a predicable and consistent beat.

The following is a chart to help you differentiate between brain states and determine the beats per minute associated with each state and the

Brain Scan	Wave	Beats per Minute
	Beta Waves- Decision Making, Logic, Problem Solving, Productivity, Motivation	**70 +**
	Alpha Waves- Listening, Reading, Peak Concentration, Thinking	**60-70**
	Theta Waves- Relaxation, Creativity	**40-60**
	Delta Waves- Deep Relaxation, Sleep	**Below 40**

Why not use music to evoke the brain state that is best suited:

- To enhance reflection, journal writing, absorption of a new learning objective or a calming effect after PE class?

- Classroom management or for changing activities?

- Perhaps music could be played in the halls while students change classes or walk to and from an assembly. This strategy may just cut down cut down on numerous behavioral problems. It's certainly worth a try!

- Accomplishing subtle influences, such as setting the tone for learning or discovery by choosing particular pieces of music to play prior to or during learning periods.

One more thought. Consider the impact of using music to calm the nerves of your students before a major test, particularly for major examinations such as your state's standardized testing or those important SATs? Who knows? Perhaps a little Mozart is all that it takes to improve test scores and thrust an entire school district into elevated status in the nation's school rankings. *What an interesting idea!*

Music as a Powerful Educational Tool

I have always used music in my classroom. I found it an excellent tool for teaching. I loved taking educational facts and setting those to simple songs. I once set to music an entire historical time line that covered explorers, the revolutionary war, the industrial revolution, the civil war, and the world wars. I can still see my students singing to the tune of Baby Face.

United States, no longer are we the United States

A division it is taking place,

In the United States,

The south wants slavery,

The north says it shouldn't be

My students even learned the order of the presidents by singing their names to the tune of "One Little, Two Little Indians."

I once received a letter from a junior in high school whom I had taught years earlier when she was in second grade. Tara couldn't resist letting me know that one of the questions on her history final was to name four presidents in order of their presidency. She wrote:

> *"I think I was the only one of my friends who got that question right. I just sang the song you taught us 9 years ago and I knew the answer! I wanted to let you know that I remembered!"*

If you teach older students, it is not necessary for you to write your own music. Let your students enjoy the opportunity!

Give them an assignment to put the educational facts to song. Divide them into groups and let them "run" with this assignment. **YOU WILL BE AMAZED BY WHAT YOUR CLASS REMEMBERS!**

I discovered music could act as a wonderful "cover" while my students were split up into small groups for one-on-one discussion. I was able to observe livelier conversation between students if I had music playing in the background than if I did not have music playing.

In order to obtain additional action research to test my observation, I asked colleagues if they would also play music while their students were involved with a similar activity and record what they observed. Unbelievably, they noticed that the level of conversation increased when music was playing. They also noticed that students were more relaxed.

I decided to ask my students to write why they felt more at ease and talked more when music was playing. They told me that they believed the music wouldn't let anyone else hear what they were saying. So, they tended not to worry if what they were saying was incorrect since their classmates had more difficulty overhearing individual conversations.

Obviously, once all of this was disclosed, I realized I reduced the level of concern among students who now realized that they might be overheard, and this allowed them to feel "safer" to engage in conversations. If you use this strategy, please remember to use music without lyrics. You don't want sing-a-longs or any songs that may not have appropriate lyrics. Also, keep the music at a soft level.

Music can be linked to memory through emotions. I don't need to present scientific studies to prove this point to you. I bet if you think of three songs that had special meaning in your life and began to sing those songs, you would return to the moment those songs became special AND the feelings you had originally associated with the music. I know that when I hear my wedding song, it triggers the mix of joy, anticipation, and a little bit of terror that I felt that day and various visual recollections such as my walking down the aisle and seeing my friends.

One of my graduate students created an emotion to memory link through music when she taught a history lesson on slavery. She brought a song to class with a slow melody written in a minor key. Then, she elicited from the students the types of emotions they felt while listening to the song. The teacher connected these emotions to what the slaves might have been feeling. Empathy was established and, more importantly, there was a personal connection made to the learning objective.

This strategy is universal. Use it for characters in literature, explorers, scientists, or historical personalities by asking students to bring in songs that would represent the personalities of these individuals and the mood of the times.

Connecting Music to a Subject Area

Use music to prepare for a particular subject area for your in class by establishing a song for math, science or history, for example, or playing the "subject" song just before you begin your lesson. In time, when the students hear the song, their minds will begin to engage for the upcoming subject and you will find students physically preparing to learn the subject area by taking out homework, textbooks, or notebooks. Music with a quick paced rhythm is great for prompting the class to change activities in cases such as this. When the music is turned off the class will not only be ready to engage in the learning episode, but they will know it is time to focus on you. And the best part of this is that *YOU DIDN'T HAVE TO SAY A THING!!*

If you are teaching history, you could use music to compare and contrast the present with some other point in history. Each time I taught a new time period in history, I would play a musical piece written during that period. I would also ask a student to bring in a song that was popular that day.

The students would then create a Venn diagram to compare and contrast the words of the song, instruments, beats, theme or emotions of both pieces of music. The students not only found this engaging, as it kept them active in their learning, but they were also able to retain the lessons they learned about certain historical events.

The same strategy works for other subject areas. For example you could do the same thing to prepare a literature lesson. Play songs that were popular during the life of an author or songs from a particular story setting. The possibilities are endless!

A word of caution: Make sure the popular songs students select is appropriate for your class.

Music as Patterns and Beats

Don't forget! Music consists of sounds, patterns and beats. One of my favorite activities is to create sounds for learning objectives.

I remember teaching a science unit on the Rain Forest. One of my inspirations was to divide my students into groups and have them create a presentation consisting of sounds that represented the Rain Forest. After each group presented its assignment, I asked the students to list on paper what they might find in the Rain Forest. They provided excellent answers.

After all, in order to create the sounds, the students had to have learned everything about the Rain Forest. What fun we had! Here are some suggestions for you to create your own sound presentation:

- Create the sounds of the city and the country.

- Create the sounds you might have heard crossing the ocean on the Mayflower.

- Create the sounds you might have heard if you fought in the Battle of Gettysburg (or any other battle).

- Create the sounds of a flower growing.

- Create the sounds of Elizabethan England.

Teachers tend to shy away from using music in the classroom. The main reason is that teachers believe they need to carry a tune or play an instrument in order to use music as a tool.

Rosemary Dolinsky

Remember, music consists of sounds, patterns and beats! This should help you expand its uses to accomplish your teaching objectives.

Try it!...YOUR STUDENTS WILL THANK YOU.

~6~

The "Color" Connection

During the years I spent as a classroom teacher, I attended many workshops where I wished I had an alarm clock to wake me during the breaks, just before lunch, and when the workshop was over. I am sure all of you were participants in one or two professional development seminars in which you also thought, "When will this day ever end?" When I started conducting workshops of my own, I promised myself not to drive others to this level of misery. My audiences were going to remain energized and responsive throughout my entire presentation! So, to keep this resolution, I created a "bag of tricks" to accompany my presentation materials.

I remembered hearing about the corporate "power dress." Dark suit. White shirt. Red tie. This area of executive dressing was new to me. Don't forget, I was a teacher! I had no need for power dressing to close the deal. As a teacher, I focused on having my students remember my lesson objectives even if it took sitting on the floor in a learning circle for that to happen. No power dress for me!

Now I felt it was time to consult with people who had expertise in the "power dressing" field. I located Gloria Starr (gloriastarr.com), Developer and CEO of Global Success Strategies, Inc. Established in 1983, Global Success Strategies, Inc. is recognized as a leading authority on impression management. Based in Toronto, Canada, Ms. Starr offers an "executive finishing school" to help "movers and shakers" dramatically increase their visual presence, maximize their communication skills, and improve their levels of performance. In order to advise me of correct colors and style, it was important for Gloria to understand the message I wanted to convey to my audience. I explained to her that it was necessary that the audience recognize me as a peer, yet identify me as the leader of the workshop. Gloria chose blacks and shades of reds and purple for me to wear.

These colors offered the correct physiological and psychological effects I hoped to create. They would act like a magnet and draw the audience's attention to me as the authority figure. As an added bonus, these selections complemented my skin tones. I looked good!

Now, I was on the right track. I knew what to wear as a seminar facilitator that would help me accomplish my goals. However,

I still didn't know **why** I had to wear these particular colors to realize these goals. How would **these** colors work to captivate my audience as opposed to other colors? My natural curiosity about the physiological activity and learning prompted me to study the reaction of the brain to color. That eventually lead to my "aha" moment when I truly understood the importance of color to my presentation, and the need to add to my "bag of tricks" what I had learned about it!

That "aha" moment brought new meaning to a comment my interior decorator had made when he decorated my new home. Lenny LaBeur remarked that he was going to weave the colors that I love into the selection of new furniture to create my desired ambience in my home. Lenny was using color therapy. *I hadn't known!*

Research suggests there are enough universal reactions to color and mood to make color a powerful accent to use in the classroom. However, it is important for you to understand that **using color is not going to take the place of good teaching techniques.** Just as decorating a room with beautiful colors is not going to hide a torn sofa, adding color to your presentations, changing the color of your bulletin boards, color dressing for different lesson objectives, or painting your classroom walls is not going to hide poor planning, content, or delivery.

Before I offer suggestions to enhance your ability to incorporate color into your teaching, I must "fix the tires" by explaining color and related brain activity. So, let's begin with a description of modern color theory and a definition of color. Then, I will offer specific ideas regarding the use of color in your classroom.

The Study of Color

Fascination with how color affects our moods, health and thought processes have a long history. In ancient Egypt, healing temples were built where a patient was bathed in specific colors of light to produce different effects. However, the foundations of modern color theory truly began with the scientists of the seventeenth century. Sir Isaac Newton's famous prism experiments were the first to reveal light as a mixture of all the colors of the visible spectrum. His finding was reinforced by studies that proved that colors recombined to form white light when the seven-color band passed through a reversed prism.

In the years following these revelations, a number of scientists made additional discoveries:

> • Johann Wolfgang von Goethe, a German writer, was the first person to describe the psychological effects of color and to identify the three primary colors: red, blue and yellow. He studied color for over twenty years before publishing *Zur Farbenlehre* (Theory of Colors) in 1810.

• Edwin Babbitt was a major influence of color in the 19th century. Babbitt explored what is now known a chromotherapeutics, the use of color and healing. It was in 1878 that he wrote *Principles of Light and Color*.

• Ghadiali Dinshah, a naturalized American from India, laid the foundation for the modern study of color. His work is probably the most extensive and detailed of any this century. Dinshah worked for many years researching the effects of color, developing colored filters and lamps and applying his scientific knowledge to the application of color in physical disease. His science was soundly based on the discoveries of Goethe and Newton. In 1933, he wrote *The Spectro Chrometry Encyclopeida* that laid the foundation for subsequent studies of color.

• Dr. Harry Riley Spitler, during the same time period as Dinshah, developed what is known as "Syntonics." A branch of ocular science used clinically for over 70 years in the field of optometry, Syntonics is the study of the physiological and psychological reactions in patients made by changing the color of light that enters the eye.

I can remember learning the mnemonic device ROY G. BIV to learn the order of the colors in the spectrum as a student in school. I also recall that the order of the colors is constant and that each color has a "signature" or wavelength to identify its location. These wavelengths are really subtle vibrations. One of the jobs of our eyes is to detect these reflected vibrations and transmit this information to the brain. The brain then interprets the color by the number of vibrations. Red has the longest wavelength and the slowest vibration. On the other end of the spectrum, violet has the shortest wavelength and the fastest vibration.

See below.

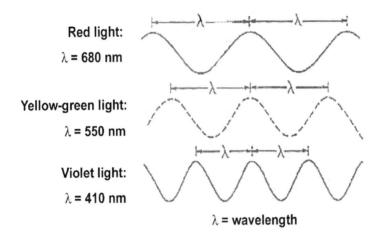

Red light:
λ = 680 nm

Yellow-green light:
λ = 550 nm

Violet light:
λ = 410 nm

λ = wavelength

The human body reacts to the vibration of color emotionally, psycho-logically and physically. How does it do this?

Experts believe the physical and emotional response to color is chemical. Scientists who study color believe that not all vibration signals reach the brain. They believe some signals are sent to the pituitary gland. The pituitary gland is central to our wellbeing. It is the master gland of the entire body. It produces (secretes) many hormones that stimulate glands in the body to produce other hormones or to complete certain actions. For example, when a person is exposed to red, a chemical signal goes from the pituitary gland to the adrenal glands and adrenaline is released. This occurs in a fraction of a second.

Let's look at some detailed physiological responses pertaining to some of the more popular colors.

RED

Physiological Effects:

• Raises blood pressure and rate of breathing.

• Improves appetite by sensitizing taste buds.

• Stimulates autonomic nervous system which leads to quick decision.

Research Has Shown:

• Restaurants often use red as a decorating scheme because of its ability to stimulate appetite.

• Rooms accented in red can cause people to lose track of time so bars and casinos favor this color.

BLUE

Physiological Effects:

• Releases eleven tranquillizing neurotransmitters.

• Slows down pulse rate.

• Deepens the breathing.

• Suppresses appetite.

Research Has Shown:

• Students score higher in blue colored rooms.

• Some weight loss programs advise dieters to use blue plates when serving meals.

• do not decorate with blue because it suppresses appetite.

YELLOW

Physiological Effects:

• The first color people distinguish when looking at an object.

• Adds to stress by preparing a person for flight or fight.

• Speeds metabolism.

• Most eye-fatiguing color, (light reflected by its bright color results in excessive eye stimulation and irritation).

Research Has Shown:

• Yellow rooms cause babies to cry more often.

• Adults tend to lose their tempers more often in yellow rooms.

GREEN

Physiological Effects:

• Has a neutral effect on the nervous system.

• Is the easiest color on the eye.

• Reduces perspiration.

Research Has Shown:

• The suicide rate dropped 34% when the color of London's Blackfrair Bridge was changed from black to green.

BROWN

Physiological Effects:

• Promotes the synthesis of serotonin.

• Stimulates the formation of prostaglandin E! (A hormone like substance in the tissues and the body fluids significant for overall normal functioning).

Research Has Shown:

• Children are less hyperactive in a brown room.

PINK

Physiological Effects:

• Releases norepinephrine, a chemical that inhibits the specific hormones that contribute to aggressive behavior.

Research Has Shown:

• Some prisons have experimented with painting their wall pink to reduce aggressive behavior. The American Institute for Biosocial Research in Washington reported that when prison cells were painted pink (bubble gum pink), it reduced aggressive behavior among prisoners. The presence of pink reduces the probability of angry or aggressive behavior even if a person is so inclined. The reactionary capabilities of the heart muscles are significantly reduced. It's a tranquilizing color that saps energy.

Please keep in mind that individuals will have different reactions to color because of personal associations. For example, even though red may be known to excite, it could actually calm a child who associates this color with something soothing, for example, a red teddy bear or "cuddle blanket."

Color Code Your Classroom

Refer to the chart below to help you make decisions on color coding your classroom.

For Alertness Use	For Creativity Use	For Reflection Use	For Relaxation Use
Black	Light Blue	Beige	Green
Orange	Jade Green	Soft Pink	Pale Brown
Purple	Yellow/Gold	Rose	Light Green
Red	Orange		Light Pink
	Purple		White
	Red		Peach
			Grey

Lorraine O'Rourke, a fifth grade teacher in New Jersey, has experience applying these color principles to her class. She dresses for work keeping her daily lessons in mind. She explained:

"If I am testing my students, I wear blue or green. Or, if I want their full attention, I wear orange or shades of red or purple."

What a novel to way to add another dimension to dressing for work! You can enhance your teaching objectives while wearing the outfit you love.

I can visualize a clothing store in the mall just for teachers.

Instead of being organized by the type of clothing, it would be organized by lesson objectives. As you walked in, there would be signs that lead you to "Testing" or "Journal Writing Day" outfits.

Imagine a line of clothing in roses, greens and blues! If you needed an outfit to teach a creative writing lesson, you would look for the area of the store with the red, orange and purple attire with the bold patterns. Perhaps some of us could take up a second career as a Teaching Store Consultant!

Martha Corwin, a first grade teacher, emailed me another interesting idea. She wrote: *"Since taking your workshop, I have tried to incorporate many of what you call "above and beyond" strategies into my lessons. My students, parents, and I are having so much fun using color. I sent a letter to the parents (on peach colored paper) explaining the power of color. Also, I created a color dress code according to the most important activity of the day. For example, if the students are going to be tested in a particular area, it is assessment day. The children take a note home that simply states "ASSESSMENT DAY." The parents have the color chart at home and the students come to school dressed in relaxation colors. Not only does each of my students now know all the colors, but I really believe I am using today's research to give the children every opportunity to succeed. Thank you!"*

The Interior Design of the Ideal Classroom

Most teachers don't have input on the choice of colors for classroom walls or flooring. However, if you do, I would like to help you create a classroom that is aesthetically pleasing and may help to achieve your particular teaching objectives.

Let's start with walls. Please avoid white. It is better to use pale relaxation colors such as light green or blue. If you have a reading area, use cushions with simple designs of peach, rose, light brown. If you have a rug in this area, be careful about using a bold design. It may look pretty but the children may have a hard time sitting still and concentrating, reading a story or listening. You are much better off using the greens, blues, roses, peaches and beiges.

Matching Colored Paper to Objectives

I have visited many schools and have noticed the photocopy areas of offices and teachers rooms. All the paper is white! When placing orders for paper supplies orders or purchasing reams of paper at stores, it is just as easy to split your order into ones for different colors. There is seldom a difference in price. Doing this will help you to accomplish a specific objective:

• Need to print out a test? Pick up the light green or blue paper.

• Want to create an assignment sheet? It's time for a little orange.

• What about a creative writing activity? It is simple to create a master sheet with lines on your computer. Photocopy this sheet onto red paper and get those creative juices flowing!

Parents always get anxious if their child hands them a note from the teacher. Why not reduce their anxiety by using a progress report made from "relaxing" paper that is a rose or peach color? Also, a reminder could be on a sheet of "alert" paper that is yellow or orange. Color—will it make a difference in your classroom?

I have presented the evidence and now it is up to you to decide by performing your own action research!

~7~

The "Connection" Connection

I would like you to look at the words I have listed below.

1. Tunnel   7. Snow White

2. Twins   8. Roller Blades

3. Baseball   9. Whip

4. Automobile   10. Bowling

5. Hand   11. Train Track

6. Worm   12. Roses

If I gave you one minute to memorize all of these words, and ask you to recall, not only the order, but the number that corresponds to each word, (e.g. the number nine and whip) in an hour from now, would you be able to do so? Think you can't? I know you **CAN**, and I will show you how.

People who succeed in this task are individuals who have mastered remembering. Actually, there are two very important *Look, Visualize, Connect* strategies you need to know and teach your students. The first *Look, Visualize, Connect* should be used when the objective is to have your students memorize basic recall information. You know, where a student must start at the bottom in learning tree (knowledge) before it is possible to move to higher thinking skills.

The second *Look, Visualize, Connect* strategy is essential to make information personal and meaningful to the individual learner. This is the strategy that is used when students take correct brain compatible notes.

Look, Visualize, Connect Strategy - Number One

Let's begin with a word list. I can remember teaching a specific science lesson to my fifth grade class. I was introducing the body joints: hinge, sliding, ball and socket, fixed, and pivot. Very basic activity, but my students needed to know the names of the joints before I could move up the learning tree from just learning the information to assigning a higher level task of creating a new body joint and explaining its function.

If my students did not know the ***Look, Visualize, Connect*** strategy, I can say with 100% accuracy that not every student would have succeeded with even the basic memorization of the names of these joints. However, I took the time to "get out of the car and fix the tires." I spent an entire lesson just showing my students **how** to implement this strategy before teaching them the actual content. By the time I introduced the joints, it took less than 6 minutes for ***EVERY*** student to learn these names. How do I know? I timed it and not one, *I repeat*, not one student missed naming the five joints on the final test!

Before knowing how to memorize the list correctly, my students were most likely to use straight memorization. That is, they were more likely to simply take sections of the list and repeat each section over and over until they had memorized them. Then, they would have proceeded to add another section and another section until the list was complete. This is a very risky strategy for storing information into long-term memory.

What will work is for your students to connect something already in long term memory to the new learning. Sounds backwards, right? But, you need to have a memory to create a memory! So remember, when you are trying to teach something new, it is imperative you connect it to something already learned.

Now, look at the twelve words I introduced to you at the beginning of this chapter. Please remember, these are hand picked words. I chose words that would have easy connections in order for you to completely understand this strategy.

• The first word is *Tunnel*. Tunnel is next to the number one. See the picture of a tunnel in your mind. Doesn't tunnel look like a number one? There's your connection.

• The second word is *Twins*. This has an easy connection to number two. There are two children in a set of twins.

• The third word is *Baseball*. How might you connect baseball to number three? It is very important that you make **your** connection. The connection must be personal and have meaning to you. Otherwise, there is no importance attached to the learning and the learning will not be successful! Maybe for baseball, you used three strikes or three outs for your connection.

•The fourth word is *Automobile*. I have three possible connections for word four: four tires, four cylinders, or four doors. What is yours?

• The fifth word is *Hand*. Easy. Five fingers on a hand.

• The sixth word is *Worm*. Do you see a possible connection to the number six? I used this word in my fifth grade class. One of my students noticed that when a worm crawls around on the ground, it sometimes squiggles its body into a six. Another student used the six inch worm as his connection. There is no right or wrong connection.

• The seventh word if *Snow White*. Seven has a memorable association: Snow White and the Seven Dwarfs. There are eight wheels on a pair of roller blades and, also, you can skate into a figure eight. So, word eight connects to roller blades.

I am sure all of you have this strategy down pat by now. See how easy it is? I invite you to look at the rest of the words. Discover your own connections. Once you made those connections, do something else. Then, after an hour, take out a piece of paper and write the words on the list as originally instructed. What may have seemed impossible at first will now seem like child's play.

Let me take you back to the lesson I taught on the five joints. I wrote the names of the joints on the chalkboard in random order. Since my students knew what to do, I wasted no time explaining the strategy. Immediately, I asked my class to create connections as a group. The class came up with a list they were each able to recall.

•The first joint was *Hinge*. A student noticed that the door hinge of the classroom looked exactly like the number one.

• The second joint was *Sliding*. We concluded a sliding door slides two ways. Also, a person is able to slide back and forth.

• The third joint was *Ball and Socket*. Ball and "Soccer" was the choice for the third joint. Since my students also knew the main list you learned, we used the same association for the word *baseball*, but shortened it to the word Ball from the game soccer. The class formed the connection by recalling that you need a ball to play soccer and associating soccer with socket.

• The fourth joint was *Fixed.* I told a story about ***fixing*** dinner for (four) my family.

• The class thought of five men on a basketball team who pivot when playing and the fact that there is a letter "IV" in the word pivot and the word five.

Your brain is capable of learning as many of these lists as you want to learn. The sky's the limit!

Classroom Use Suggestions

There are many students who have trouble with multiplication. Try the following recommendation. Let's say the problem is 7 X 8 = 56. Take Snow White, which is the seventh word, create a flash card of her on roller blades, word 8, skating on 56th Street. You may have the students create a whole set of flashcards using multiplication facts. Now, they will remember that seven times eight is equal to fifty-six!

I believe by now you trust the fact that making connections when memorizing information is a powerful way to remember and it works! It, therefore, makes sense to use this strategy as often as possible when you are looking for automatic responses. Teaching the correct operation to use when working with math word problems is always a challenge for some students. Being able to look at the key words and initiate the operation they represent, that is, addition, subtraction, multiplication, or division is the automatic response you are hoping will occur. I can help transform your hope into reality.

First, create a class color for each operation. For example, decide that blue stands for addition, red for subtraction, green for multiplication, and purple for division. Create a simple chart of the colors and their associated operations and hang it on the wall for referral. Now, every time you write a math problem on the board, use the color chalk specified for each color to write the operation. Therefore, if you are writing 5 x 3 = 15, write the X in green. If you are writing 19 + 2 = 21, write the + in red. Ideally, your students should have magic makers and repeat this activity every single time they write an operational sign. Secondly, give your students a list of key terms that also indicate the operation used to solve the math problem. Then, have your students color code each phrase.

The chart below illustrates some key terms that might be used. Add the colors you will use to code them. You should also think of others to supplement this list.

Key Term	Underline or Highlight With:
How many altogether?	Blue
What is the total?	Blue
How many more?	Red
What is the difference?	Red

When you first begin using this strategy, the students will *LOOK* at the phrase, *VISUALIZE* the color, and make a *CONNECTION* to its corresponding operation. Eventually, the color coding will no longer be necessary and you can eliminate this step completely.

This color connection does not have any limitations. You may use this strategy for any area of teaching. One of my graduate students decided to do her own action research. She color-coded the word "Spring" *red* when writing a poem on the chalkboard for her Pre-K class. She read the poem each morning for a week as she usually does with each poem she writes on the board. At the end of the week, the teacher erased the board, drew a red line on the board, and asked the class which word she had written in red.

The class was able to respond with the correct answer, "Spring." She again wrote the word without the color coding, and she asked if anyone were able to read the word. Without hesitation, the students could read the word. Needless to say, my graduate student was impressed!

Below I have offered other ways to use coding in:

• *Grammar:* Make nouns orange, verbs purple, adjectives gold, and adverbs blue. Then code and write the definitions in the same colors.

• *Geography:* Make rivers red, mountains brown, continents purple, and oceans blue. Color code the names of rivers, mountains, continents, and oceans in the same colors.

• *Sequential order:* This is helpful when students need to follow steps, especially in science or with mathematical computations. A red check is always first, a blue check second, an orange check third, etc.

• *Creative writing papers:* Use different color paper for each step of the writing process.

• *Organizational activities:* Cover morning books with white book colors, afternoon books in blue covers. Or just stick a circle dot on the binding of the books for students to see.

Also, do not worry about using the same color for different activities. The connections will still happen.

Look, Visualize, Connect Strategy - Number Two

Look at the six words listed below.

Clown   Envelope   Hunter

Desk   Children   Computer

I want you to look at each word, close your eyes, and see a picture of the word in your "mind's eye." This is your personal picture. Let's start with the word *clown*. Describe what your clown looks like to you. What is it wearing? What is it doing? At this moment you are giving personal meaning and sense to the word clown. This procedure allows attachment of a past connection, something you know about a clown, to the actual word you need to memorize. Now, do the same exercise with each word. Close your eyes and visualize. Once you have mastered this technique, you will understand the importance of creating a personal attachment to store information in memory.

This second ***Look, Visualize, Connect*** is a tremendous strategy to teach to your students. It is the backbone of taking brain compatible notes. This strategy should be taught when note-taking skills are first introduced to students. This usually occurs in the third or fourth grade. However, those students who do not take notes can still benefit from this second strategy as you will see after I provide you with recommendations for taking notes.

How to Take Notes

Below is information about the Roman Empire. I am going to ask you to read the information and as you do so, take simple notes on a separate sheet of paper exactly the way you have taught your students to take notes. Then, put your notes aside and continue reading the rest of this chapter. When you have completed the chapter, reread the selection and take notes using my instructions. Compare the two types of note taking. I am sure you will agree with me that the note taking strategy I have suggested to you is extremely effective. Here's your passage:

The Origins of the Roman Empire

In AD 114 you could travel from Scotland to the Sahara desert and still be within the Roman Empire. Given the technology of the time and the fact that nearly two thousand years later we are still trying to unite Europe into one government, it is perhaps true to say that the Roman Empire has been one of man's greatest achievements. The Romans took their empire and gave it one government, a common language and one currency, something which the politicians of today can probably only dream of accomplishing.

We still use the Roman alphabet, Roman numerals and Roman months. The Romans developed concrete, glass windows, the dome, central heating, blocks of flats, public health, public baths, hospitals, a postal service, a fire brigade, a civil service and international trade. Roman roads, aqueducts and buildings still survive and Latin - the language of the Romans formed the basis of most of the European languages including Italian, French, Spanish and English. Latin is even taught in many schools even though it has been a "dead" language for many centuries. But where did it all start? Well, there are perhaps two answers to this question, as any historian can tell you. We can look at the facts and try and work out what the evidence shows us.

Indeed, archaeological evidence suggests that Rome began in about 1600 BC as a collection of small round wooden huts built on a group of seven hills near the river Tiber on the borders of Etruria in central Italy. There is, however, another version of the creation of Rome and one which the Romans themselves convinced themselves was true.

I have chosen to explain the most effective note taking technique by modeling the strategy for you and explaining it within the model. However, before you review carefully my "class notes" on the next page, I want you to remember to teach note taking skill in isolation from your lesson objective. Give your class the opportunity to fully understand the **how** and **why** they must take notes in this manner.

Again, trust me. The extra time you take to do this will be well worth as the end results will show.

When you begin teaching technique or if you are teaching students who need extra space, I suggest you use two pages of the notebook. The right notebook page is used for your information. The left notebook page is used for the visual or word connections. For those teachers whose students do not take notes, try this: As you are presenting information to the class, stop every few minutes, and ask the class to close their eyes and visualize what was just said. At this point, you may have the students:

- Turn to each other and explain what picture was in their "mind's eye."

- Keep a visualization diary where they draw their "mind's eye" each time they are directed to do so.

This note taking skill is very effective. When the subject of how notes is taught as a separate lesson and then incorporated into everyday class-room activities, you have added a study skill strategy your students will use through grammar school, middle school, high school, and college.

Key words, Visual, Mind Map

Cook

In Narrow Section

Review with Flash

The notebook page should be folded or divided just as you see this page...

-one wide section.

-one narrow section.

Note taking is very similar to making dinner. First you need to gather the ingredients. Then, you cook the meal. When your students take notes, the ingredients consist of:

ALL THE INFORMATION YOU EXPECT YOUR STUDENTS TO KNOW!

This information is written in the wide section of your students' notebook page. Once the ingredients (information) are in the notebook, it is time for your students to start "cooking" and get their brains to remember. This is really simple to do. Ask your students:

To read the information in wide section. What do you "see" in your mind as you read?

Tell them: What you "see" in your mind, whether pictures or key words, place in the narrow section of you notebook page. *What you see WILL BE different from what others see.*

They are giving meaning to the information side of the notes. They are making the information very personal which will help them remember.

The pictures and words used were mine. Perhaps these pictures would be different for you. To easily review terms and begin drilling, immediately make flash cards and practice using individual learning styles.

~8~

The "Right/Left Brain" Connection

In my workshops, I want educators to be cognizant of the fact the brain is divided into two distinct hemispheres, and each hemisphere has "assigned" specific functions. I want teachers to understand the importance of these functions in order to develop teaching strategies for each student. Therefore, I begin each workshop presentation quite dramatically by asking everyone to look around and notice that there is no agenda anywhere with the daily schedule.

There are for a few reasons to begin my presentations by asking the participants to do this. First, I am an extremely right brained dominant individual and following a schedule is difficult. You see, even though I know what needs to be covered and what I have to do, I may not know the precise order in which it will be covered. I am not good at following any sequential order. Secondly, if the schedule states that lunch is at 12:00 and I am still talking at 12:06, the *Sequentials* in the room will start looking at their watches. Or, if I have deviated from the designated topics, these participants will want to know why have not stuck to the agenda.

At this point, I can usually see some discomfort on some faces of people sitting in my audience. I know from experience these are these are my Left Brainers i.e., Sequentials, who need to know step by step what will be occurring throughout the day. I usually let them know that I realize I have raised their level of concern by omitting a schedule. I remark to the others in the workshop that they can also recognize these individuals by noticing their open legal pads and readiness to take notes. Also, I mention that if you can't find your pen or pencil, these are the people to ask. They will always have extras!

 I recall one teacher, Irene Sura, who teaches at Pope John Paul II School in Clifton, NJ. After attending my brain based workshop, she wrote me the following which always brings a smile to my face:

> "*I am an organized, everything-in-its-place person, right down to having attended your workshop with a rubber band tightly encircled around my pens and markers. When you good naturedly kidded me about being a left-brained learner at the beginning of the workshop, I was astounded that you would know this when we had never met each other prior to that day. Yet, when we*

teachers were later asked to test our hemispheric preference, I learned from the results that I indeed am a left-brained learner."

I must add that by the end of that workshop, Irene had taken all her markers out of the rubber band and had scattered them on the table. She told me that she was willing to become a ***right brainer!*** Irene has since participated in other workshops I have presented, and we still laugh about her markers.

Hemispheric Preference Needs Recognition

Right or left brain preference is an area of brain research that needs to be recognized in our schools and kept in mind when lesson plans are created. Of course, in my workshop presentation, I use a caricature style to separate the hemispheric functions. I need a humorous hook to get my participants to examine closely what is going on in the left and right sides of the brain. I must remind you that the brain is complex, and I am simplifying the processes to help you focus on some key points.

Also, I must ask you never to use the left brain or right brain individual preference as the sole explanation of a student's behavior or thinking process. For example, never **categorize** a student as a right or left brain learner and use that as a reason why he or she is not creative or logical. Functions of the brain are **not exclusive to just one side**. Each side of the brain "talks" to the other side. The two sides of the brain work together for harmony and greater understanding of whatever situation began the processing. Remember one hemisphere may be more active but both hemispheres compliment each other in almost all activities.

Discoving Hemisphericity

Right and left brain specialization was discovered before the development of technology to scan the brain. During the 1950s doctors began to experiment with cutting the corpus callosum, the cable or nerves that connects the two hemispheres of the brain, in order to stop seizures. The cutting of the bridge separating the left and right side of the brain meant each side of the brain could no longer "talk" to the other. The experiment showed such encouraging results when performed on monkeys with epilepsy that it was ready to be tried on humans in the early 1960s.

Although the surgery resulted in the considerable reduction of seizures, doctors had no idea what effects cutting the corpus callosum would have on the individual's lifestyle. After surgery, the patients appeared "normal." They walked, talked, read and played sports. Only after the careful "split brain experiments" of Roger Sperry, Michael Gazzaniga and Joseph Bogen, did we begin to understand the real effects on a human when visual and tactile information is presented to the patient's left or right side of the brain without the other side knowing. The results of those experiments were astounding!

To present visual information to one hemisphere or the other, doctors used a tachistoscope, which flashes an image in a specific part of the visual field so fast that the subject does not Have time to move his or her eyes. In one experiment, a word (for example "fork") was flashed so only the right hemisphere of a patient could receive the information. The patient would not be able to say what the word was. However, if the subject was asked to write what he saw, his left hand would begin to write the word "fork." If asked what he had written, the patient would have no idea. He would know that he had written *something*, he could feel his hand going through the motion, yet he could not tell observers what the word was. Because there was no longer a connection between the two hemispheres, information presented to the right half of the brain could not convey this information to the left.

Interestingly enough, the centers for speech interpretation and production are located in the left hemisphere. Similarly, if the patient is blind-folded and a familiar object, such as a toothbrush, is placed in his left hand, he appears to know what it is; for example, by making the gesture of brushing his teeth. But, he cannot name the object to the experimenter. If asked what he is doing with the object, gesturing a brushing motion, he has no idea. However, if the left hand gives the toothbrush to the right hand, the patient will immediately say "tooth brush".

Scientists have continued to perform split brain experiments. As scientific equipment has become more sophisticated, so have the results. By transferring this medical information into teaching information, we now can create strategies for the classroom based on established research.

Following pages is a chart that outlines the responses and functions of the right and left brain hemispheres of the brain.

Left Brain Learners	Right Brain Learners
Sequential	Intuitive
Detail Oriented	Insightful
Logical	Random
Concrete Thinkers	Abstract Thinkers
Responds to Verbal Directions	Responds to Demonstrated Directions
Prefers Multiple Choice Tests	Prefers Open Ended Questions
Prefers talking and writing	Prefers drawing & manipulating objects
Controls Feelings	Emotional

Looks at Differences	Looks at Similarities
Values Words Spoken	Reads Body Language
Solves Problems by Organizing Data	Solves Problems by Visual or Verbal Clues
Looks at Parts	Looks at the Wholes

Keeping the specialization of the brain in mind, you will be able to plan your lessons with more understanding of brain compatible strategies and add another component to teaching and meeting the needs of all your students.

Below, I have presented a starter checklist of strategies to be used in your classroom. As you continually research brain based keep adding to the list with personal strategies that work for you. I purposely did not separate the list into left or right Brain activity since I want you to think of teaching to the "whole brain".

Remember to:

• Create webs, Venn diagrams, spider maps.

• Create a general outline of lesson objective whether written or verbal.

• Break tasks into smaller parts with a deadline for completing each part.

• Use hands-on learning.

• Have a routine or system for accomplishing a task.

• Give options for an assignment.

• Use memory strategies such as mnemonics or peg words to remember details.

• Time assignments.

• Use metaphors as an analytic strategy.

• Ask "what is" questions to stimulate logical thinking.

• Set goals when assigning tasks to complete.

• Attach emotions to the learning episode.

• Relate personal experiences to new knowledge.

• Use color to focus on specific details and facts.

• Have the students write summaries.

• Relate new material to prior knowledge

.

~9~

The "Awareness" Connection

As I drove my new car out of the showroom, I was positive I was the only one in the whole world who was driving a car like this one. I pictured other drivers staring at me wondering about the type of car I was driving and where I had found one so beautiful.

This car was mine and mine alone, until I got to the first traffic light! As I was sitting in the car waiting for the light to turn green and thinking about how everyone was admiring my new car, I watched a car cross the intersection. It was my car! Someone else had my car! I glanced in the rearview mirror and what did I see? My car! Someone else had my car! No matter where I drove that day, I saw someone else behind the steering wheel of my car! Has this ever happened to you?

I remember reading the word bagasse. I had never seen or heard this word before. It was brand new to me. Of course, I went directly to the dictionary to find its meaning. Now, I couldn't wait to use bagasse at the next appropriate opportunity, which occurred only one day later. I was having dinner with my friend, Gail. In course of conversation, I couldn't believe what came out of Gail's mouth! She used… bagasse! I wanted to shout at Gail that bagasse was my word! Was she reading my thoughts? How could she have known that word I had just learned? It was such an unusual word. I must tell you, for the next few weeks that seemed to be the only word I heard or read. Has this ever happen to you?

I am sure I could spend hours relating stories like these. They sound like coincidences, but are they? I began to wonder what could be done to use these "coincidences" in the classroom. Was there a rational explanation for what had happened to me? **There was!**

Let's take the car. I had probably seen my car on the road numerous times, before my purchase, but there had been no reason for me to take notice. I had no interest in this car UNTIL I owned one. I had raised my awareness of this model after my purchase. In other words, *I had made a personal connection through personal awareness.* The same thing happened with my new word. When I read the word, I took an interest in the word by looking up its meaning in the dictionary and deciding to add it to my vocabulary. *I had made a personal connection through personal awareness.*

I asked myself whether this concept could be used in the classroom to enhance learning. It can! In fact, I feel it is such an effective strategy, I named it: "**Personal Awareness Photography.**"

I believe that this strategy brings awareness from the subconscious memory to the conscious memory. Subconsciously, I had seen my make and model car on the road many times. I just paid no attention. And, I am sure I heard or read the word "bagasse" before. Again, I just paid no attention.

Why would you use Personal Awareness Photography in your classroom? Because it creates a *"recollection trace"* for future learning! The goal of my Personal Awareness Photography is to have your students become aware of your "up and coming" teachings without any effort on your part. All you need to do to use Personal Awareness Photography to its fullest potential is **"plant"** visuals relating to upcoming chapters, units, or lesson objectives in the classroom.

It is best to "plant" your visuals within your students' peripheral vision. I know this will be hard because of the seating configuration of the classroom, but try your best. By using the peripheral vision tactic, the information is always being **"seen"** by the brain. Now, you are subconsciously making your students aware of topics and, when watching television or reading, your students may hear or see a connection to upcoming events in your classroom.

About six weeks after ending a brain based graduate class where I discussed Personal Awareness Photography strategy; I received an email from one of the students. Jill Sposato, a 7th grade teacher in Totowa, NJ, told me she had tried an experiment in her class using the awareness connection. She said:

"I created a bulletin board with the title: 'Coming Attractions.' I knew my next unit would be the Revolutionary War. On this bulletin board, I placed posters of the war and key facts written on banners I had created with my computer. Two days after I created the bulletin board, one of my students approached me and told me she had been watching television and that the information on the bulletin board was correct! I had never discussed anything on that board, yet my student made a learning connection. Thank you, Rosemary. This strategy worked!"

Of course, it is important for me to give you research to support this strategy. A study made by the Department of Neurobiology at Harvard Medical School, made in conjunction with the Department of Psychology at Boston University, concluded that while focusing on one thing, people can learn something else subliminally from their side vision. These findings, which appeared in *Nature* magazine, stated that a person can focus on one thing, like television, and absorb information in their peripheral vision. So even when the mind is not paying attention to extraneous information, it ends up processing that information. These studies could have a tremendous impact on teaching techniques and layout of educational environments in the future.

The Harvard/Boston study was conducted on students who were asked to look at a computer and identify letters that flashed rapidly across the screen. Half of the participants sat next to a separate screen, displaying grey dots, much like the visual snow on a television set with bad reception. About five percent of the grey dots were moving in the same direction, a pattern that was barely discernable to the naked eye.

Later, both groups were tested on their ability to look at a television screen and detect any pattern of moving dots. The group that only had one screen within its field of vision could not detect moving dots, even when ten percent of these dots marched in the same direction. But everyone in the group who had been exposed to more than one screen of moving dots had an enhanced ability to detect a pattern.

If you like the idea of Personal Awareness Photography to help your students remember the information presented in your lessons, I have another powerful strategy for you to implement in your classroom using the same principal. I also want you to teach your students this strategy to use at home.

Create flashcards with highlights of your lessons. I suggest the flashcards contain both pictures and words. If you are a primary teacher, you may write up to three informational facts on the cards. If you are a middle or high school teacher, don't use any more than five informational facts on the cards. Tape these flashcards in places around your room where students visit frequently. (i.e., above the light switch, pencil sharpener, the paper supply table, computer station, reading corner, etc.). Then forget about them. Each time, students see the cards, they will glance at the information, and their brains will subliminally absorb what has been written or drawn on them.

To teach your students to use Personal Awareness Photography as a study technique at home, give them a "creating their own flashcards assignment" using the information taught in your lesson. Ask them to tape the cards around their home where there is a probability they will frequently view the cards such as the mirror they use, the refrigerator, etc. Instruct them to go about whatever they are doing and pay no attention to the cards because *their brain will be paying attention!*

~9~

Final Thoughts

In 1889, Thomas Smith, a London businessman, offered advice to advertisers concerning the number of exposures a consumer needed before purchasing a product. Remarkably, marketing agencies still think the advice is applicable today. Now, I believe we could connect that same number of exposures in the marketing world to the number of revisits a teacher must make to information in order for that information to be stored into our students' long term memories.

Therefore, I took some instructive liberty with Mr. Smith's "consumer exposures to buying products" advice and turned it into "teaching exposures to remembering information."

Rosemary Dolinsky

	Marketing	Remembering
Exposures	People	Students
The 1st time	...don't even see the ad	...don't even see or hear the information.
The 2nd time	...don't notice it.	...don't notice it.
The 3rd time	...are aware that it is there	...are aware that it has been mentioned.
The 4th time	...have a fleeting sense that they've seen it somewhere before.	...have a fleeting sense that they've heard it somewhere before.
The 5th time	...actually listen.	...actually listen.
The 6th time	...thumb their nose.	...try to ignore it.
The 7th time	...start to get a little irritated with seeing it again	...start to get a little irritated with hearing it again
The 8th time	...start to think, "Here's that confounded ad again	...start to think, "Here's that confounded thing again
The 9th time	...start to wonder if they may be missing out on something	...wonder if they should be paying attention because they are missing out on something
The 10th time	...ask their friends if they've tried the product/service.	...ask their friends if they know anything about the "stuff."

The 11th time	…wonder how the company is paying for all these ads.	…wonder how the teacher knows so much about this "stuff."
The 12th time	…start to think the product may be good.	…start to think it.
The 13th time	…start to feel the product has value.	…start to believe the "stuff" is interesting.
The 14th time	…start to remember wanting a product or service exactly like this for a long time.	…start to remember the "stuff."
The 15th time	…start to yearn for it and think about buying it	…start to yearn to learn more about the "stuff."
The 16th time	…accept the fact that they will buy it sometime in the future.	…accept the fact that they will need to know the "stuff" sometime in the future.
The 17th time	…have made a note to buy	…have made a note to really remember.
The 18th time	…curse their poverty for not allowing them to buy this terrific product.	…curse the fact they didn't know this
The 19th time	…count their money very carefully	…study very care study very carefully
The 20th time	…see the ad, they **BUY** what is offered	…hear the "stuff," they **REMEMBER!**

As you can see, it does take a very long time, and many exposures, to have a consumer finally purchase a product. Now, aren't you, too, selling a product in school? That product being education! So, just like the advertising industry, it is necessary to have patience and understanding that no long term learning will occur without many exposures to your learning objective.

If million dollar businesses find that Mr. Smith's advice is still relevant and it continues to work for them, it is also relevant and will works for us: *the educators*. Therefore, when you get frustrated thinking your students just "don't get it," I hope you keep "tucked way back in your mind" Mr. Smith's message and ***revisit, revisit, and revisit!***

Many years ago, my 7th grade teacher would tell the class to, "Please remember and never forget." It was our clue the information somehow would be very important to all of us. It probably would show up on a test. Using the words of Miss Schaefer, I ask you now to:

PLEASE REMEMBER AND NEVER FORGET...

- Use smell, color, hemispheric preferences, and learning styles techniques in your lessons.

- Connect the new learning to past learning.

- Dig deep into your "bag of teaching strategies" to grab as many techniques as you can to reach every child.

• Seek new techniques, strategies, and research on a regular basis.

• Keep revisiting your learning objectives in as many ways as possible

• Keep doing these things over and over and over again *and I promise you...*

NO CHILD WILL BE LEFT BEHIND IN YOUR CLASSROOM!

Bibliography

Abbott, A. Neurobiology: Music, maestro, please!, Nature, 416, 12-14, 2002.

Albers, J. The Interaction of Color Yale University Press, 1975.

Armstrong, T. Multiple Intelligences in the Classroom, 2nded. Alexandria, VA: Association for Supervision and Curriculum Development, 2000.

Begley, S. "Thinking looks like this: PET scans show the brain recalling and cogitating ." Newsweek, November 25,1991.

Birren, F. Color and Human Response, New York: Van

Nostrand Reinhold, 1978.

Birren, F Principles of Color, New York: Van Nostrand Reinhold, 1969.

Bruyn, Eds., Handbook of Clinical Neurology, vol. 4., pp. 273-290, Amsterdam: North Holland, 1985.

Gardner, H. Frames of Mind: The Theory of the Multiple Intelligences, New York: Basic Books, 1993.

Golden, D., and A. Tsiaras. "Building a better brain." Life Magazine, Vol 17, Issue 7, page 62, July 1994.

Gurian, M. Boys and Girls Learn Differently, California: Jossey-Bas, 2001.

Harman, W., & Rheingold, H. Higher Creativity: Liberating the Unconscious for Breakthrough Insights. Los Angeles: Jeremy P Tarcher, 1994.

Hirsch, A, Life's a Smelling Success: Using Scent to Empower Your Memory and Learning, New York: Authors of Unity, 2002.

Jensen, E. Music with Brain in Mind, California: The Brain Store, 1996.

Kotulak, R. Inside the brain: Revolutionary Discoveries of How the Mind Works. MO: Andrews McMeel.

Marem, M. "Productivity: The surprising science of workplace effectiveness." Success, September 1991.

Moss MC, Scholey. Oxygen administration enhances memory formation in healthy young adults. Psychopharmacology 124: 255-260, 1996.

Morton Walker, The Power of Color, New York: Avery Publishing Group, pp. 50-52, 1991.

Nassau, K. The Physics and Chemistry of Color, New York: John Wiley, 1983.

Nash, G. Creative Approaches to Child Development with Music, Language, and Movement. New York: Alfred Publishing Co., 1994.

Novey, D. Clinician's Complete Reference to Complementary & Alternative Medicine, New York:Mosby, 2000.

Rauscher, F.H., Shaw, G.L., & Ky, K.N. Music and spatial task performance. Nature, 365, 611, 1993.

Rose, C. Accelerated Learning. New Your: Dell, 1980.

Rose, S. The Making of Memory. New York: Doubleday, 1992.

Silver, H., Strong, R., & Perini, M. Integrating learning styles and multiple intelligence, Educational Leadership, 55(1), 22-29, 1997.

Skurka, N. The New York Times Book of Interior Design and Decoration. New York: Quadrangal Books, 1976.

Sousa, David. How the Brain Learns, California: Corwin Press, 2001.

Sperry, R. Brain bisection and consciousness. In Eccles, J.(Ed.) How the self controls its brain. New York: Springer-Verlag.1996.

Steele, J., 'Brain Research and Essential Oils' Aromatherapy Quarterly, Spring 1984.

Stein, H. Visualized note taking: Left-right brain theory applied in the classroom. The Social Studies. July-August, 1987.

Sylwester, R. A Celebration of Neurons: An Educator's Guide to the Human Brain. Virginia: Association of Supervision and Curriculum Development, 1995.

Watson, A and N Drury. Healing Music: The Harmonic Path to Inner Wholeness. Bridgeport, England: Prism Press. 1978.

Wlodkowski, R., & Jaynes, J. Eager to Learn. San Francisco: Jossey-Bass. 1990.

Internet Sites

- Dana Alliance for news about the brain research:
- www.dana.org
- Journal of Neuroscience: www.jneurosci.org
- National Institute of Health: www.nih.org
- Nature Publishing Group for news in science research:
- www.nature.com

About the Author

Rosemary Dolinsky is an educational consultant and graduate instructor whose dynamic and entertaining style of presenting makes her a sought after national speaker and keynoter. Her energetic presentations are jam-packed with proven techniques to increase student achievement. A veteran teacher with over thirty years of successful experience in education, Rosemary remains deeply dedicated to bringing educators "above and beyond" ideas to create positive, significant and lasting learning experiences for their students.

The founder of The Cutting Edge Institute LLC consulting and publishing firm, Rosemary has appeared on numerous radio shows, and is the author of How to Avoid Conflicts BEFORE Your Class is Disrupted.

On a personal note, Rosemary and her husband, Billy, are parents of twin daughters, Kristen and Jill.

Contact Rosemary Dolinsky through her websites or email. rosemarydolinsky.com cuttingedgeinstitute.com

Email: rdolinsky@cuttingedgeinstitute.com

LaVergne, TN USA
02 September 2009
156794LV00009B/1/P

9 780984 134304